GREAT little ENCYCLOPEDIA

First published in 2003 by
Miles Kelly Publishing Ltd
Bardfield Centre, Great Bardfield, Essex, CM7 4SL

2 4 6 8 10 9 7 5 3 1

Some material in this book can also be found in the
100 Things You Should Know series

Editorial Director: Anne Marshall

Editors: Nicola Sail, Amanda Learmonth

Design: Debbie Meekcoms, Maya Currell

British Library Cataloguing-in-Publication Data
A catalogue record for this book is available from the British Library

ISBN 1-84236-271-2

Printed in Singapore

www.mileskelly.net
info@mileskelly.net

GREAT little ENCYCLOPEDIA

Miles Kelly Publishing

Contents

Space

Planet Earth

Science

Animals

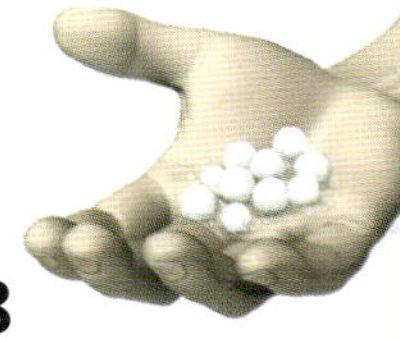

History

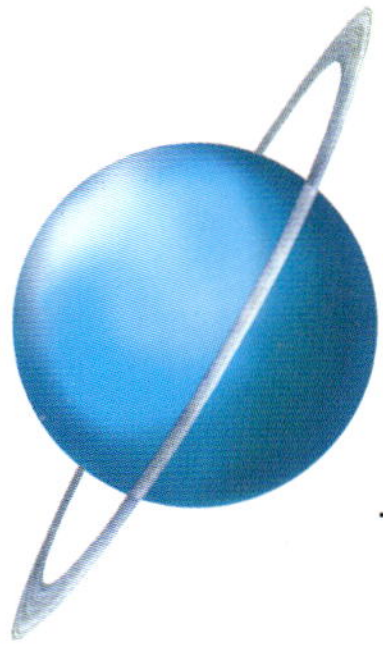

How to use this book

Read these pages carefully. They will show you how to use your book. Learn how to find fascinating information and have fun with the activities and quizzes. Don't forget to use the index at the back to find subjects you particularly enjoy!

Introduction
Every page begins with a general paragraph that will introduce you to the new topic. You will find out lots of information here.

Fun facts
Look out for the character cartoons and their wacky fun facts.

Pictures
Wonderful colour illustrations show and help you understand what you are reading about.

Activity panels
How much do you remember? Test yourself and your friends with these quizzes. You will find the answers upside down at the bottom of the panel.

Heading
You won't lose your way! Each page has a heading that shows you exactly where you are in the book.

Close-ups
Would you like to know more about what's going on in the picture? Look for these close-ups that give you lots of extra facts.

Panel pictures
These pictures provide more facts and visual information on the topic you are reading about.

Space is everywhere!

Space is all around the Earth, high above the air. Here on the Earth's surface we are surrounded by air. If you go upwards, up a mountain or in an aircraft, air grows thinner until there is none at all. This is where space begins.

▶ *In space, astronauts wear spacesuits to go outside the space shuttle as it circles the Earth.*

◀ *Space itself is mostly empty, but there are many exciting things out there, such as planets, stars and galaxies.*

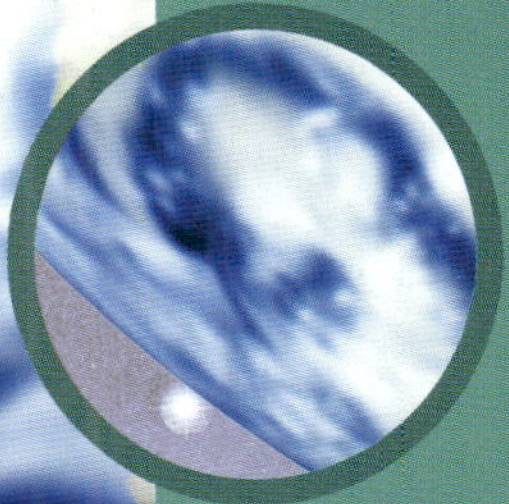

The Earth's atmosphere *is a mixture of gases that we can breathe.*

The surface of the Earth *is made up of land masses and sea.*

Astronauts *are people who travel in space.*

Our life-giving Sun

The Sun is our nearest star. It does not look like other stars because it is much closer to us. Most stars are so far away, they look like points of light in the sky. The Sun is not solid like the Earth, but is a giant ball of superhot gases. These gases are very hot and glow like bonfire flames.

▶ *The Sun's hot, glowing gas is always on the move, bubbling up to the surface and sinking back down again.*

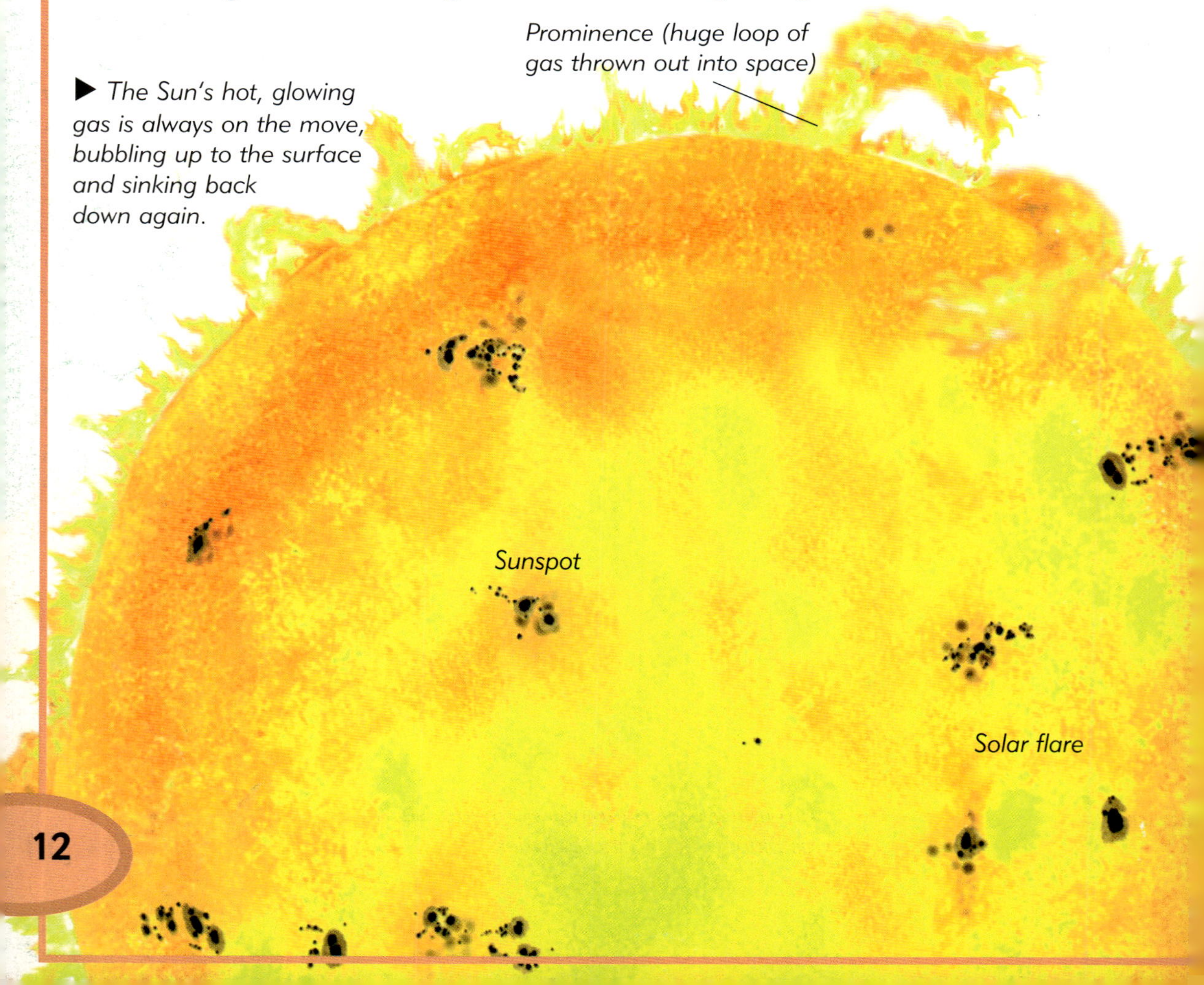

▶ *Every so often, the Sun, Moon and Earth line up in space so that the Moon is directly between the Earth and Sun. This stops sunlight from reaching a small area on Earth. The area grows dark and cold, as if night has come early. We call this an eclipse.*

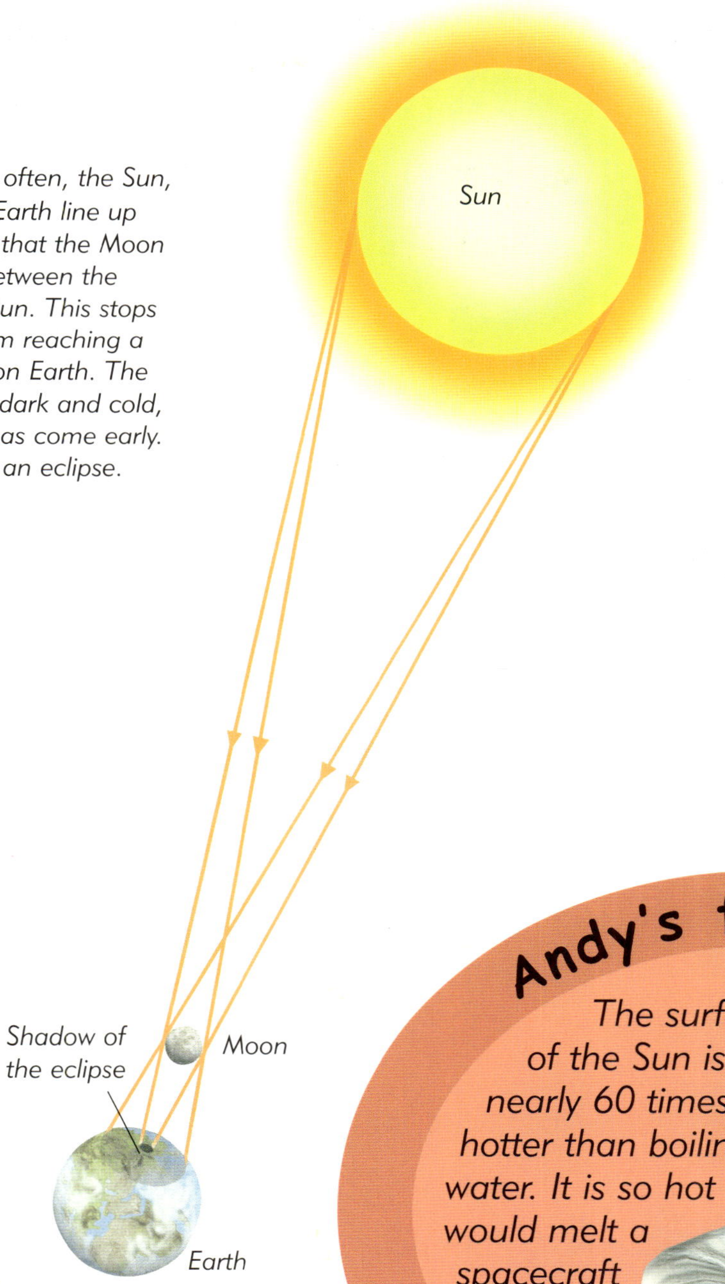

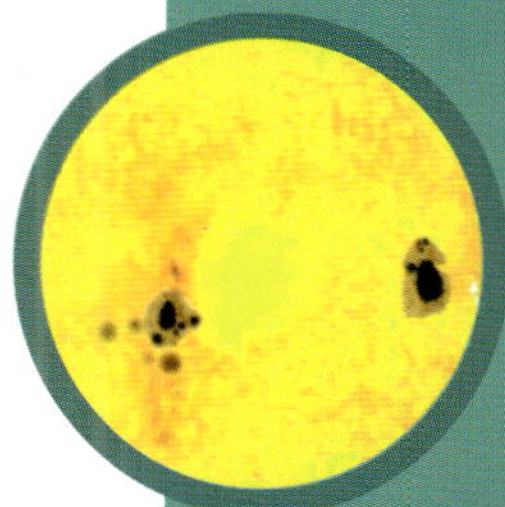

Solar flares *are explosions of energy that shoot out from the Sun.*

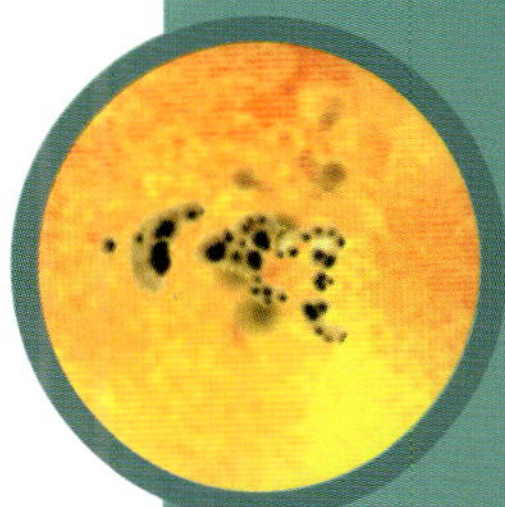

Sunspots *are massive, cooler spots on the Sun's surface.*

Andy's fun facts!

The surface of the Sun is nearly 60 times hotter than boiling water. It is so hot it would melt a spacecraft flying near it.

The planet family

The Sun is surrounded by a family of circling planets called the Solar System. This family is held together by an invisible force called gravity, which pulls things towards each other. It is the same force that pulls us to the ground and stops us floating away. The Sun's gravity pulls on the planets and keeps them travelling around it.

Some planets have rings made up of ice, dust and rocks.

From space, we can see the swirling atmospheres of the planets.

▲ The nine planets are all different. Mercury, nearest the Sun, is small and hot. Then Venus, Earth and Mars are rocky and cooler. Beyond them Jupiter, Saturn, Uranus and Neptune are large and cold, while Pluto is tiny and icy.

Andy's fun facts!

If the Sun was the size of a large beach ball, the Earth would be as small as a pea, and the Moon would look like a pinhead.

Our Earth in space

The Earth moves through space at nearly 3000 metres a second. It weighs 6000 million, million, million tonnes. Up to two-thirds of the Earth's rocky surface is covered by water, making the seas and oceans. Surrounding the Earth is a layer of gases called the atmosphere. This layer stretches 700 kilometres from the Earth's surface.

Galaxies are giant groups of millions or even trillions of stars.

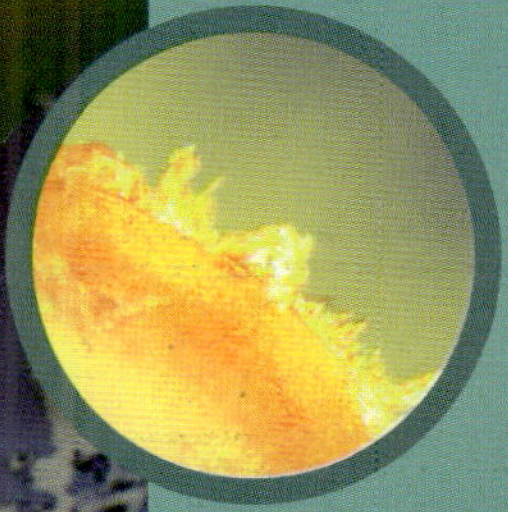

The Sun releases its energy as heat and light.

A star is a ball of very hot gas.

Earth's neighbours

Venus and Mars are the nearest planets to the Earth. Venus is closer to the Sun than the Earth while Mars is farther away. Each takes a different amount of time to circle the Sun. We call this its year. A year on Venus is 225 days, on Earth 365 days and on Mars 687 days.

◀ *There are plans to send astronauts to Mars but the journey would take six months or more.*

◀ *From space, all we can see of Venus are the tops of its clouds.*

Planet spotting

See if you can spot Venus in the night sky. It is often the first bright star to appear in the evening, just above where the Sun has set. Because of this we sometimes call it the evening star.

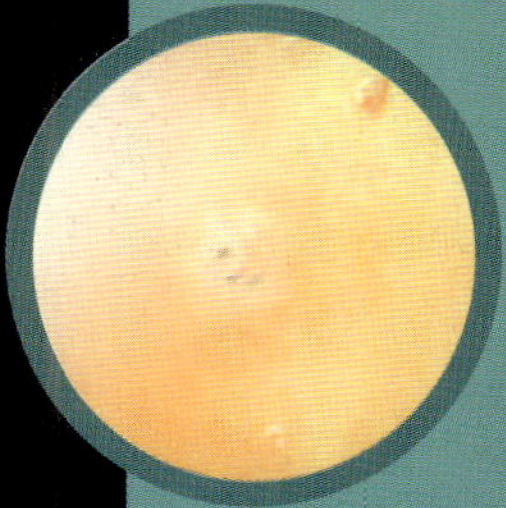

***Olympus Mons** is the biggest volcano on Mars.*

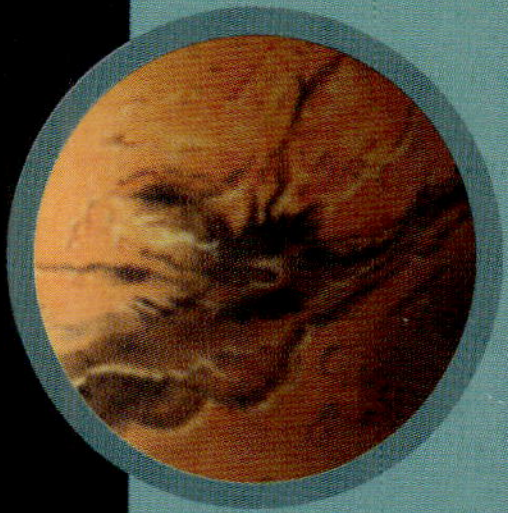

***Valles Marineris** is an enormous valley that cuts across Mars.*

***The clouds on Venus** race around the planet in just four days.*

Tiny planets

Pluto is the smallest planet – smaller than our Moon. It is so tiny and far away that it was not discovered until 1930. Mercury looks like our Moon. It is a round, cratered ball of rock. It has no atmosphere, so the sunny side is boiling hot, while the night side is freezing cold.

▶ If you were on Pluto, its moon, Charon, would look much larger than our moon does, because Charon is very close to Pluto.

Make craters

You will need:

• *flour* • *baking tray* • *a marble or a stone*

1. *Spread some flour about 2 centimetres deep in a baking tray and smooth over the surface.*
2. *Drop a marble or a small round stone onto the flour and see the saucer-shaped crater that it makes.*

▼ *Mercury has many craters. This shows how often it was hit by space rocks. One was so large it shattered rocks on the other side of the planet.*

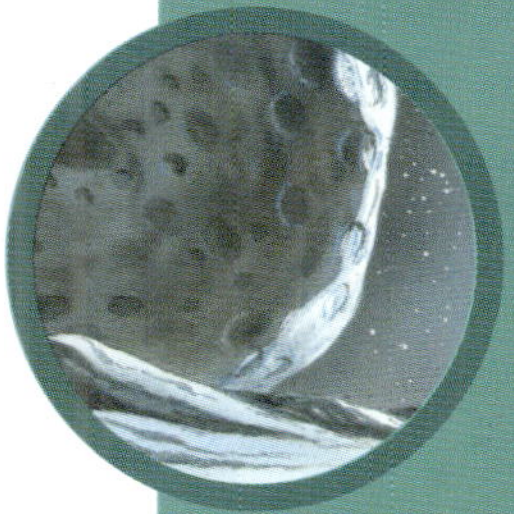

Pluto's moon, Charon, *was only discovered in 1976.*

The cratered surface of Pluto *is covered in solid ice.*

The Sun *looks huge as it rises on Mercury.*

Massive planets

Jupiter is the biggest planet, more massive than all the other planets in the Solar System put together. It is 11 times as wide as the Earth although it is still much smaller than the Sun. Saturn, the next largest planet, is more than nine times as wide as the Earth.

▼▶Jupiter and Saturn are both gas giants. They have no solid surface and all that you can see are the tops of their clouds. Beneath the clouds, the planets are made mostly of gas (like air) and liquid (like water).

▼ Jupiter's fast winds blow the cloud into coloured bands around the planet.

Andy's fun facts!

Saturn is the lightest planet in the Solar System. If there was a large enough sea, it would float like a cork.

▲ *Although Saturn's rings are very wide, they stretch out in a very thin layer around the planet.*

Saturn's shining rings *are made of millions of chunks of ice.*

The Great Red Spot *on Jupiter is a 300-year-old storm!*

Io has many active *volcanoes that change its surface.*

Far, far away

Uranus and Neptune are gas giants like Jupiter and Saturn. They are the next two planets beyond Saturn but much smaller – less than half as wide. They too have no hard surface. Their cloud tops make Uranus and Neptune look blue.

▶ *Like all the gas giant planets, Neptune is surrounded by rings.*

▼ *Most planets spin upright like a top, but Uranus spins on its side. It may have been knocked over when something crashed into it millions of years ago.*

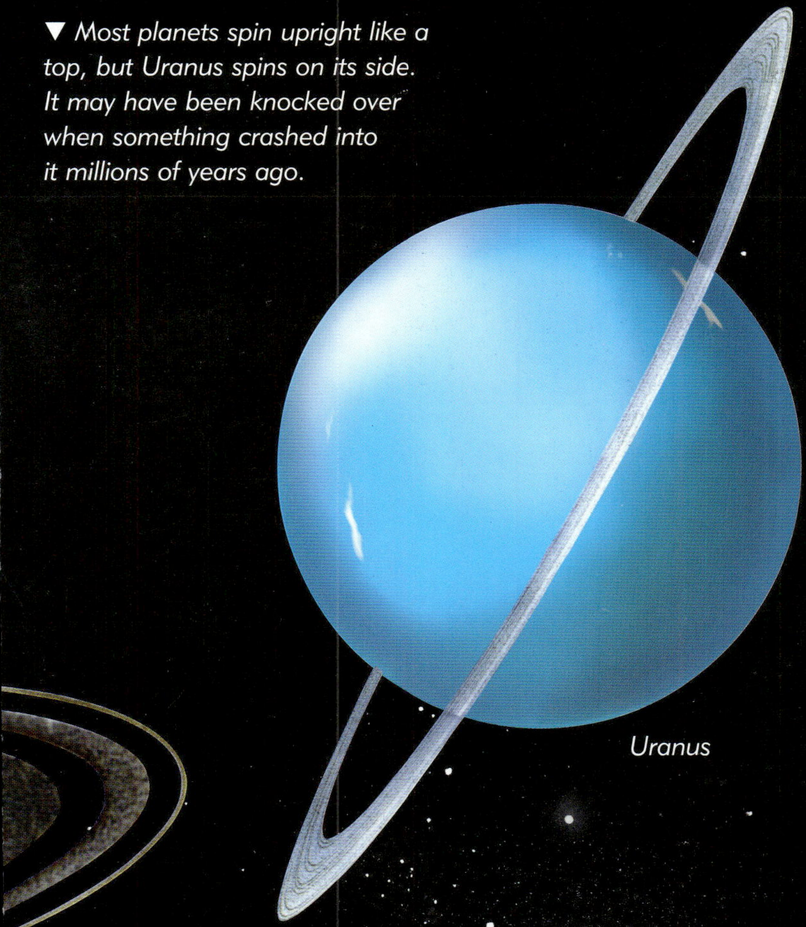

Uranus

Neptune's rings *are thinner and darker than Saturn's.*

Neptune's *bright blue clouds make the whole planet look blue.*

Uranus *is very cold, being so far from the Sun.*

Test your memory!

1. *Which is the lightest planet in our Solar System?*
2. *Which is the biggest planet in our Solar System?*
3. *Which is Earth's nearest star?*
4. *How many planets are there in our Solar System?*

1. *Saturn* **2.** *Jupiter* **3.** *the Sun* **4.** *nine*

Life in space

Space is a dangerous place for astronauts. It can be boiling hot in the sunshine or freezing cold in the Earth's shadow. There is also radiation (rays of energy) from the Sun. Dust, rocks and bits from other rockets speed through space at such speed, they could easily make a small hole in a spacecraft, letting the air leak out.

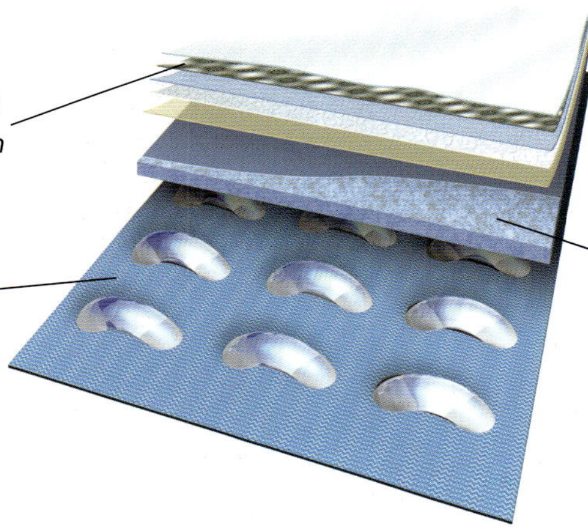

▶ *In a spacesuit, many layers of different materials are needed to keep the astronaut safe.*

Space meals

You will need:

- *dried noodles*

Ask an adult to help you. Buy a dried snack such as noodles, that just needs water added. This is the kind of food astronauts eat. Most of their meals are dried so they are not too heavy to launch into space.

▲ *Spacesuits protect astronauts when they are out in space.*

The visor *protects the astronaut's face from the sunlight.*

The joystick control *lets the astronaut move around in space.*

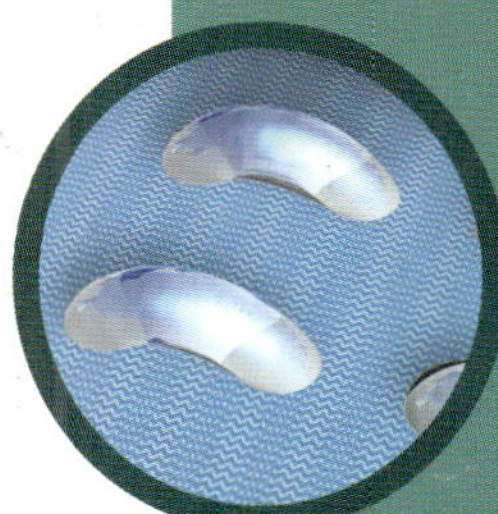

Tubes of water *under the spacesuit carry away heat.*

Off to the Moon

The first men landed on the Moon in 1969. They were three astronauts from the US *Apollo 11* mission. Neil Armstrong was the first person to set foot on the Moon. Only five other *Apollo* missions have landed on the Moon since then.

▼ *The distance from the Earth to the Moon is nearly 400,000 kilometres. That is about as far as travelling round the Earth ten times.*

▲ The Lunar and Command Modules travelled to the Moon fixed together, then separated for the Moon landing.

The Lunar Module *took two astronauts to the Moon's surface.*

The Command Module *was the same size as a car.*

The longest *time spent on the Moon was three days.*

Earth - our home

The planet we live on is Earth. It is a round ball of rock. On the outside where we live, the rock is hard and solid. But deep below our feet, inside the Earth, the rock is hot enough to melt. Sometimes this hot rock showers out of an erupting volcano.

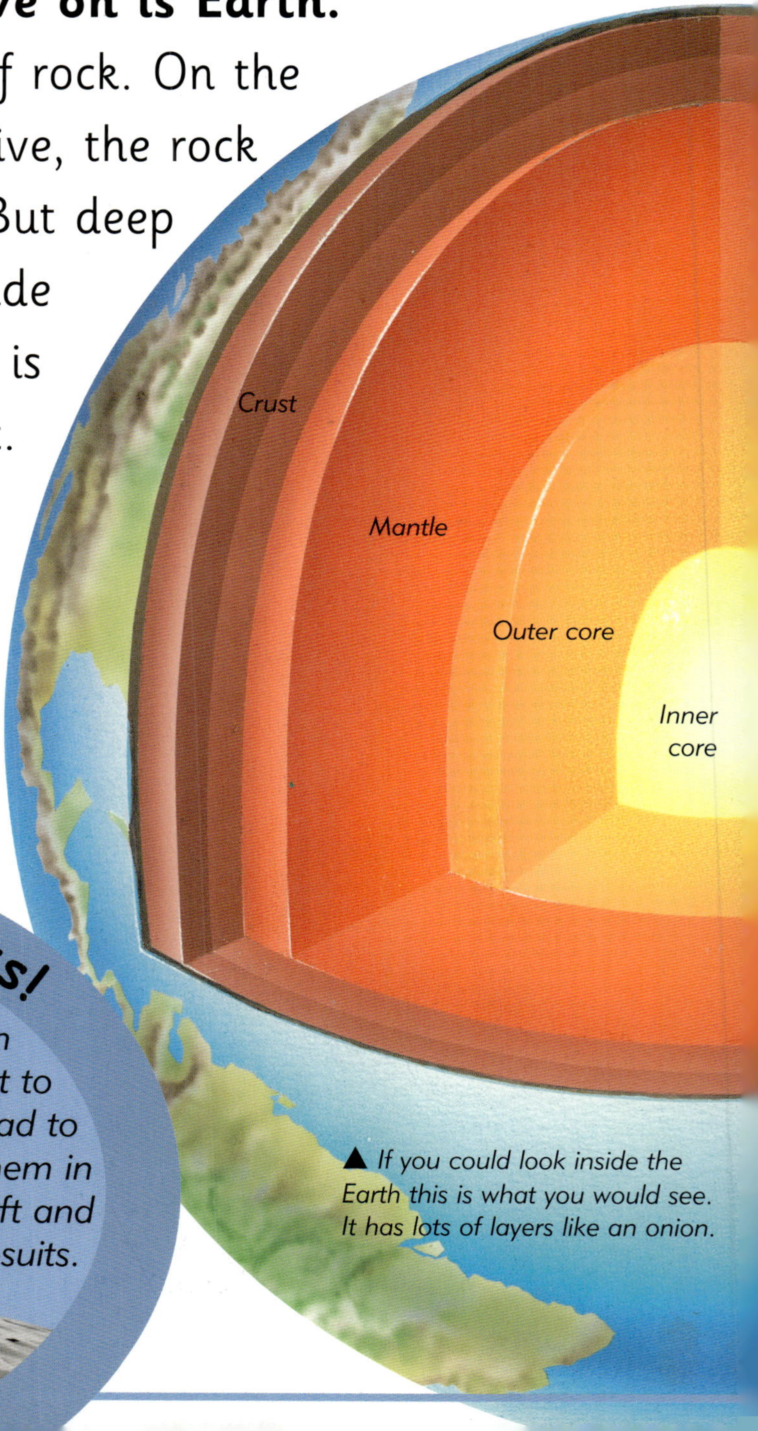

▲ *If you could look inside the Earth this is what you would see. It has lots of layers like an onion.*

Andy's fun facts!

The Moon has no air or water. When astronauts went to the Moon they had to take air with them in their spacecraft and spacesuits.

▼ *The Moon is nearer to the Earth than any other object in space. The Moon travels around the Earth, taking one month to complete its journey.*

***Craters** are scars left by space rocks that hit the Moon's surface.*

***The inner core,** at the centre of the Earth, is made of iron.*

***The crust** is the thin surface layer we live on.*

▼ *Over a month, the Moon changes from a thin crescent shape to a round shape. This is because sunlight is reflected by the Moon. We see the full Moon when the sunlit side faces the Earth. We see a crescent Moon when the sunlit side is facing away from us.*

Crescent Moon

First quarter Moon

Gibbous Moon

Full Moon

Forming the Earth

The Earth came from a cloud in space. Scientists think the Earth formed from a huge cloud of gas and dust around 4500 million years ago. A star near the cloud exploded, making the cloud spin. As it did this, gases gathered at its centre and made the Sun. Rocks, formed from masses of dust, crashed into each other making the planets. The Earth is one of these planets.

The Earth was made up of one piece of land that is now split into seven chunks, known as continents

◀ Clouds of dust and gas are made by the remains of old stars that have exploded or simply stopped shining. It is here that new stars and their planets form.

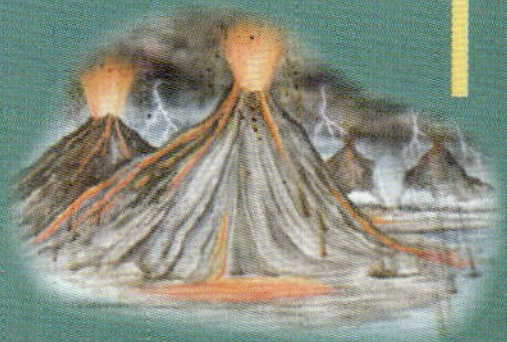

Erupting volcanoes *and fierce storms helped form the atmosphere and oceans.*

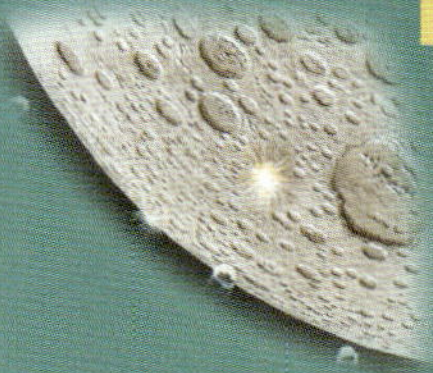

The Moon *was hit by rocks in space that made round hollows, called craters.*

Harry's fun facts!

Millions of rocks crash into Earth as it speeds through space. The larger ones that reach the ground are called meteorites.

Spinning around

The Earth is like a huge spinning top. It continues to spin because it was formed from a spinning cloud of gas and dust. It does not spin straight up like a top but leans a little to one side. The Earth takes 24 hours to spin around once. We call this period of time a day.

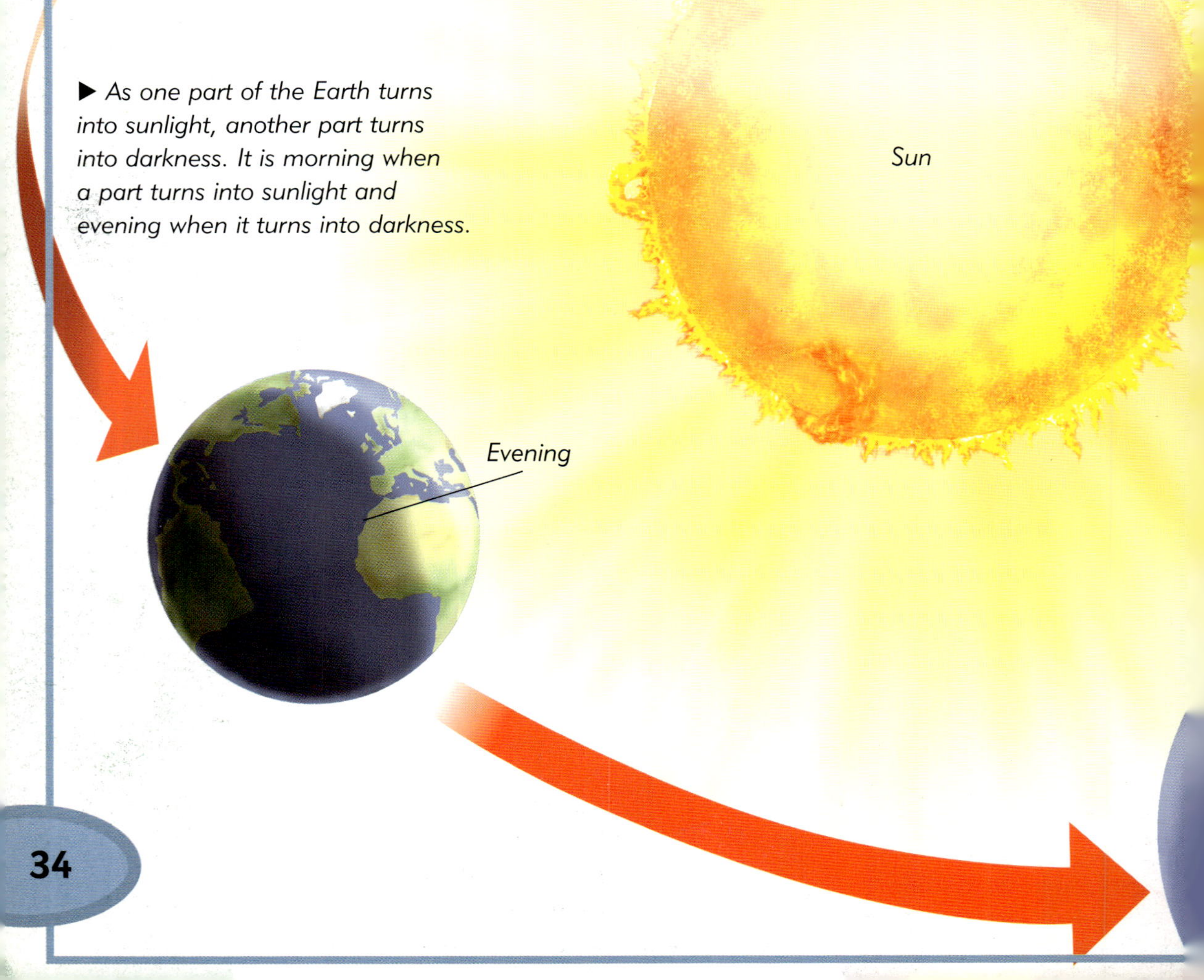

▶ *As one part of the Earth turns into sunlight, another part turns into darkness. It is morning when a part turns into sunlight and evening when it turns into darkness.*

Day and night

You will need:

- *globe of the Earth*
- *torch*

1. *In a darkened room, shine the torch at your globe. The side facing the torch (or Sun) is lit up, so there it is day. On the dark side of the globe it is night.*

2. *If you slowly spin the globe round, you will see how daylight moves around the Earth.*

◀ *The Earth moves around the Sun in a path called an orbit. It takes a year to make this journey. In that time it spins around 365 1/4 times.*

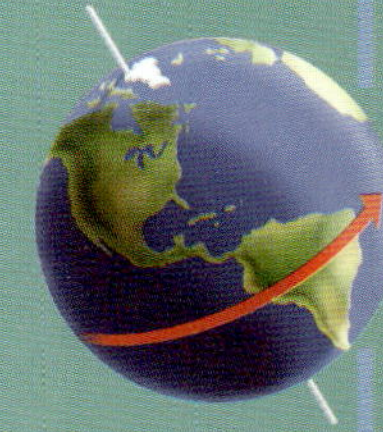

***The Earth** spins around two points. One at the top of the Earth – the North Pole. The other at the bottom – the South Pole.*

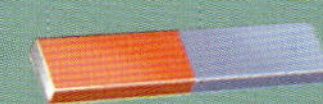

***The Earth** has a metal centre. As the Earth spins the metal acts like a magnet with two poles.*

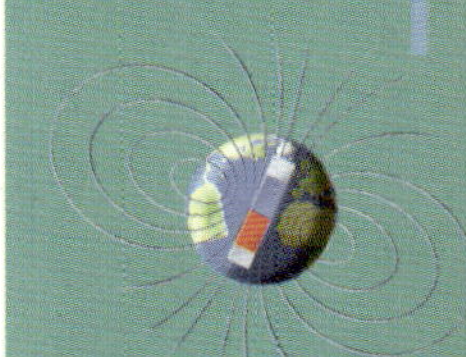

***These lines** show the pulling power of the magnet inside the Earth.*

Violent volcanoes

Volcanoes happen when hot, liquid rock shoots up through the Earth's surface. Beneath a volcano is a huge space filled with molten (liquid) rock. This is the magma chamber. Eruptions happen when pressure builds up inside the chamber.

Make your own volcano

You will need:

• bicarbonate of soda • tray
• plastic bottle • food colouring
• vinegar and sand

1. *Put a tablespoon of bicarbonate of soda in the bottle.*
2. *Stand the bottle in a tray and make a cone of sand around it.*
3. *Put a few drops of red food colouring in half a cup of vinegar.*
4. *Tip the vinegar into a jug then pour it into the bottle. The volcano should erupt with red, frothy lava.*

◀ *When a volcano erupts, the hot rock from inside the Earth escapes as ash, smoke, flying lumps called volcanic bombs and rivers of lava.*

Shield volcanoes *form when runny lava flows from the vent forming a dome shape.*

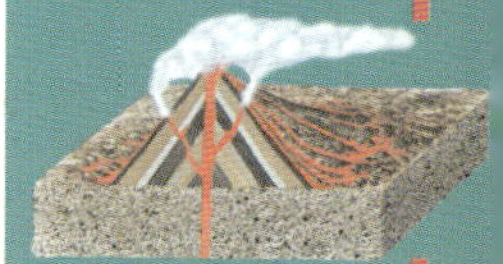

Cone-shaped volcanoes *form when ash settles on thick lava after an eruption.*

Crater volcanoes *form when a cone-shaped volcano sinks into the magma chamber.*

Making mountains

The youngest mountains are the highest. Young mountains have uneven peaks because soft rocks on the mountain top get broken down. Underneath are harder rocks that take longer to break down, but even these are worn away in time. This makes an older mountain shorter and gives its top a rounded shape.

▼ *It takes millions of years for mountains to form, and this process is happening all the time. A group of mountains is called a range.*

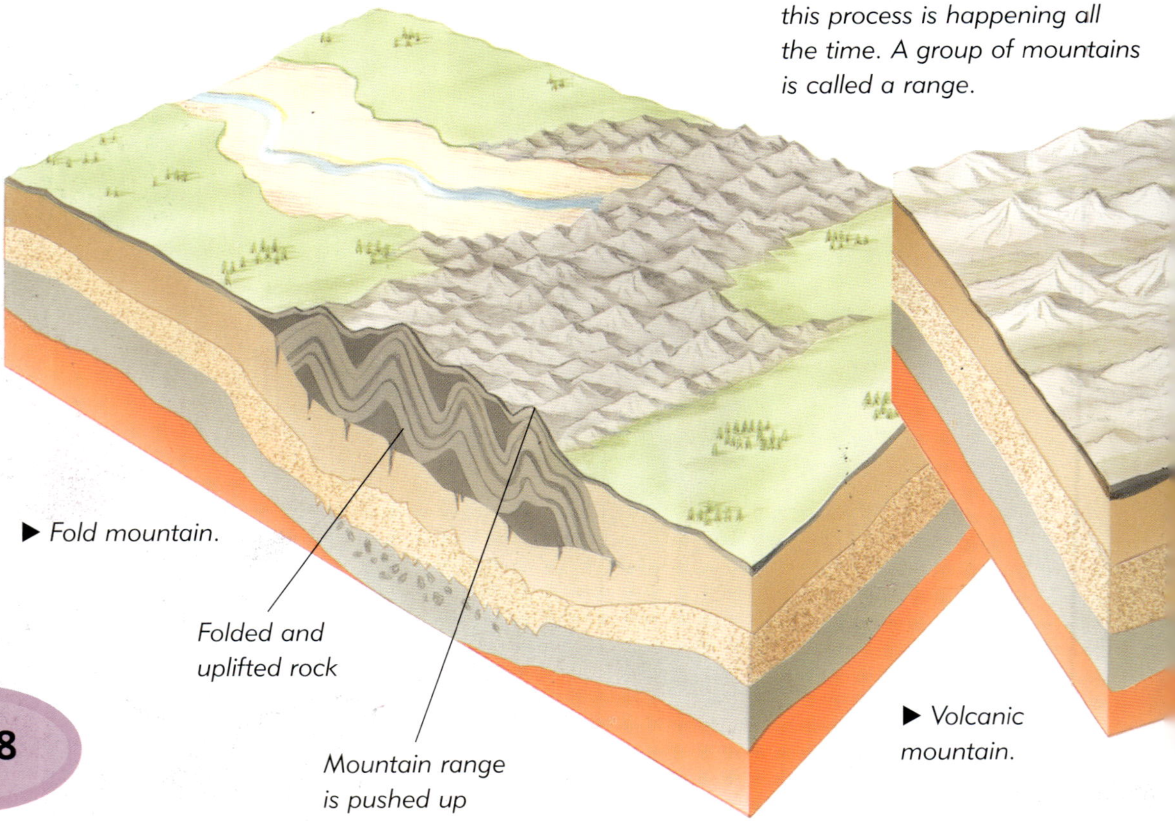

▶ *Fold mountain.*

▶ *Volcanic mountain.*

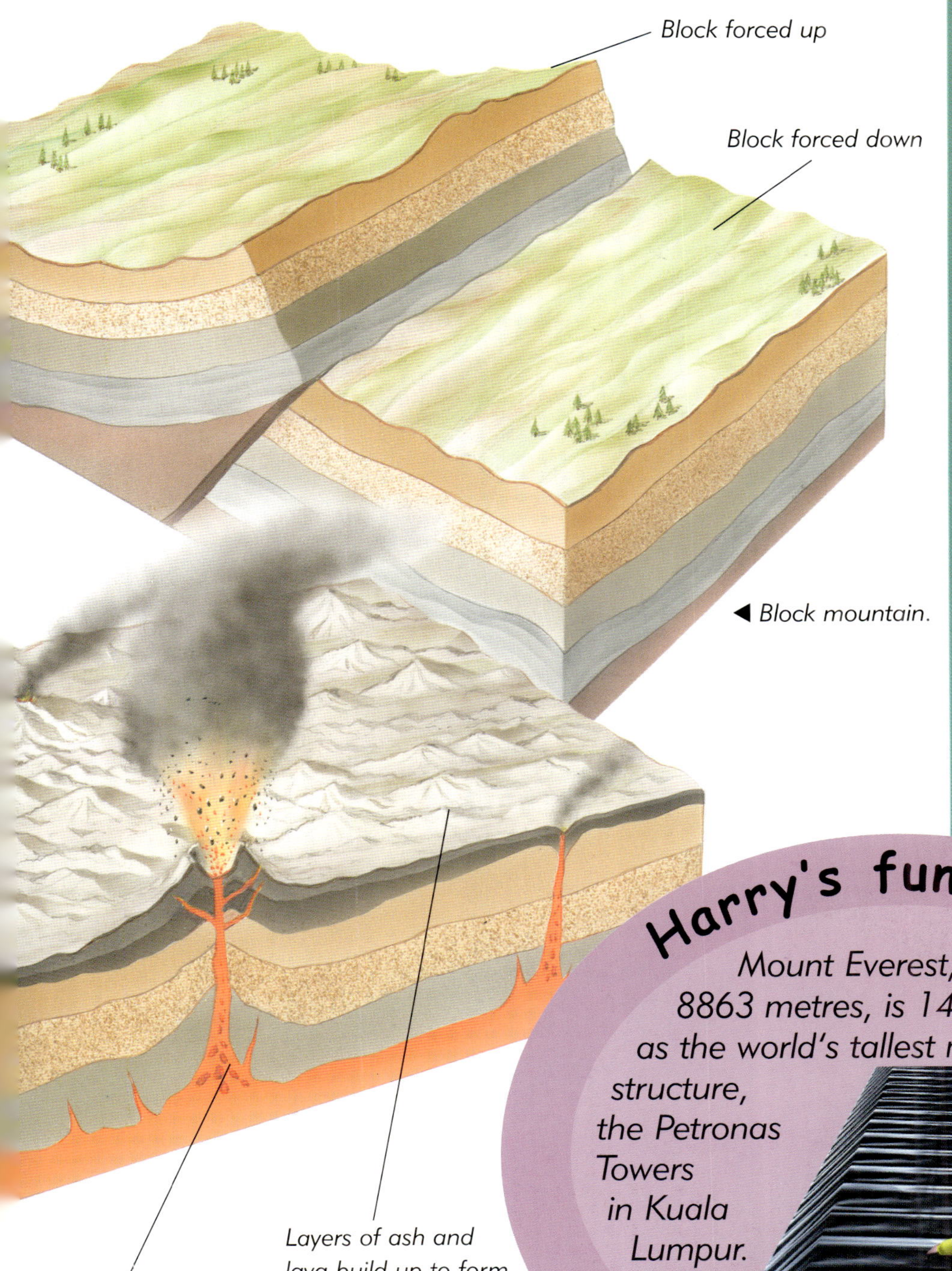

◄ Block mountain.

Some mountains are so tall that their summits (peaks) are hidden by cloud.

Mountains are the tallest natural features on Earth.

Harry's fun facts!

Mount Everest, at 8863 metres, is 14 times as tall as the world's tallest man-made structure, the Petronas Towers in Kuala Lumpur.

Shaking and quaking

An earthquake is caused by violent movements in the Earth's crust.

An earthquake starts deep underground at its focus. Shock waves move from the focus in all directions, shaking the rock. The epicentre (where the shock waves reach the surface) is where the earthquake is strongest.

Harry's fun facts!

A tsunami is a huge wave caused by an earthquake far out at sea. A tsunami can be up to 30 metres high – that is as high as a block of flats!

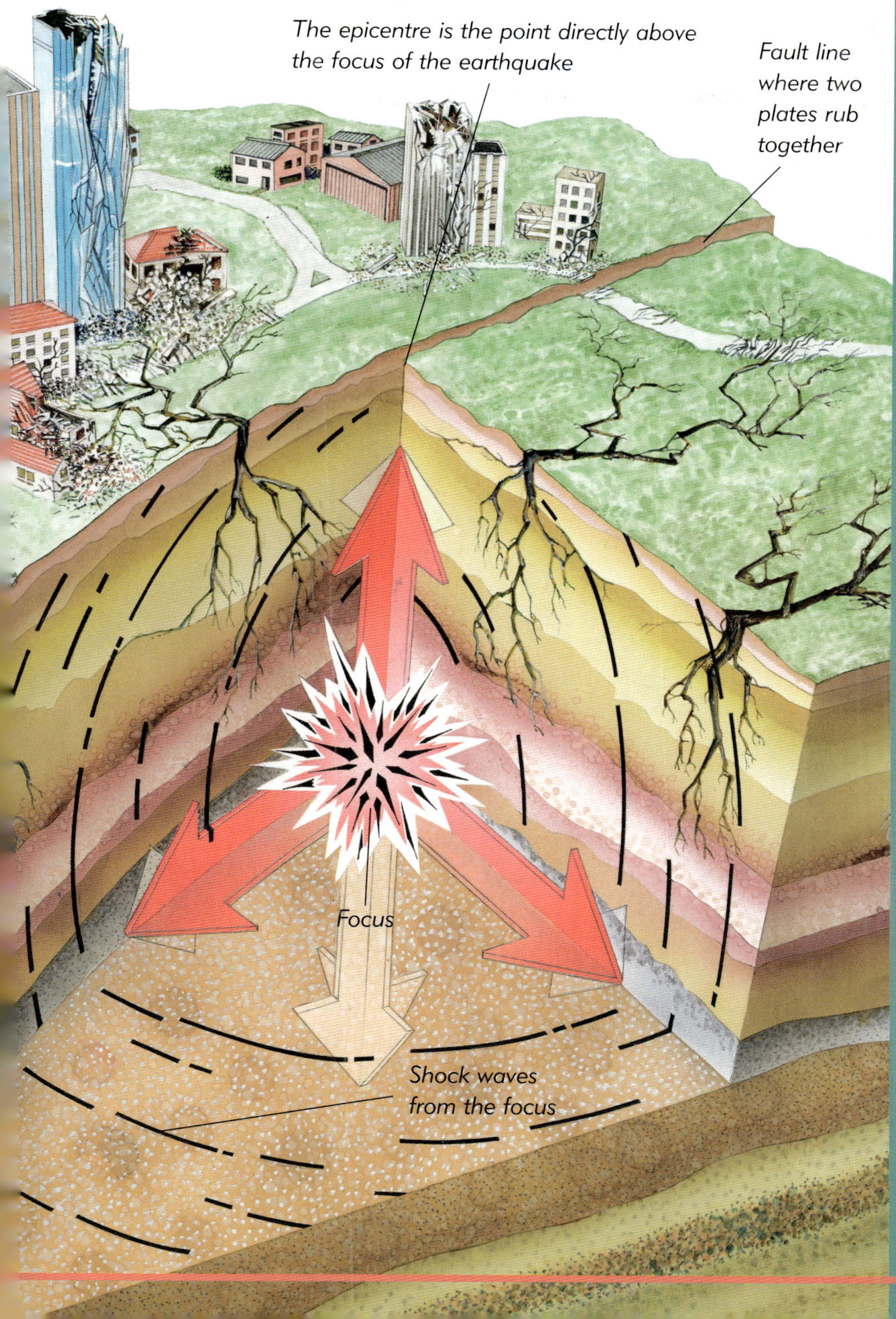

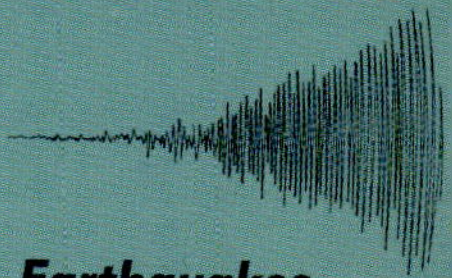

Earthquakes cause various shock waves that can be measured using the Richter scale.

Lights start swinging at level 3 on the Richter scale.

At level 5, windows break, at 6, chimneys will topple over.

Lakes and rivers

A mighty river can start from a spring. This is a place where water flows from the ground. Rain soaks into the ground through the soil and rock, until it gushes out on the side of a hill. The trickle of water from a spring is called a stream. When streams join together, they make a river.

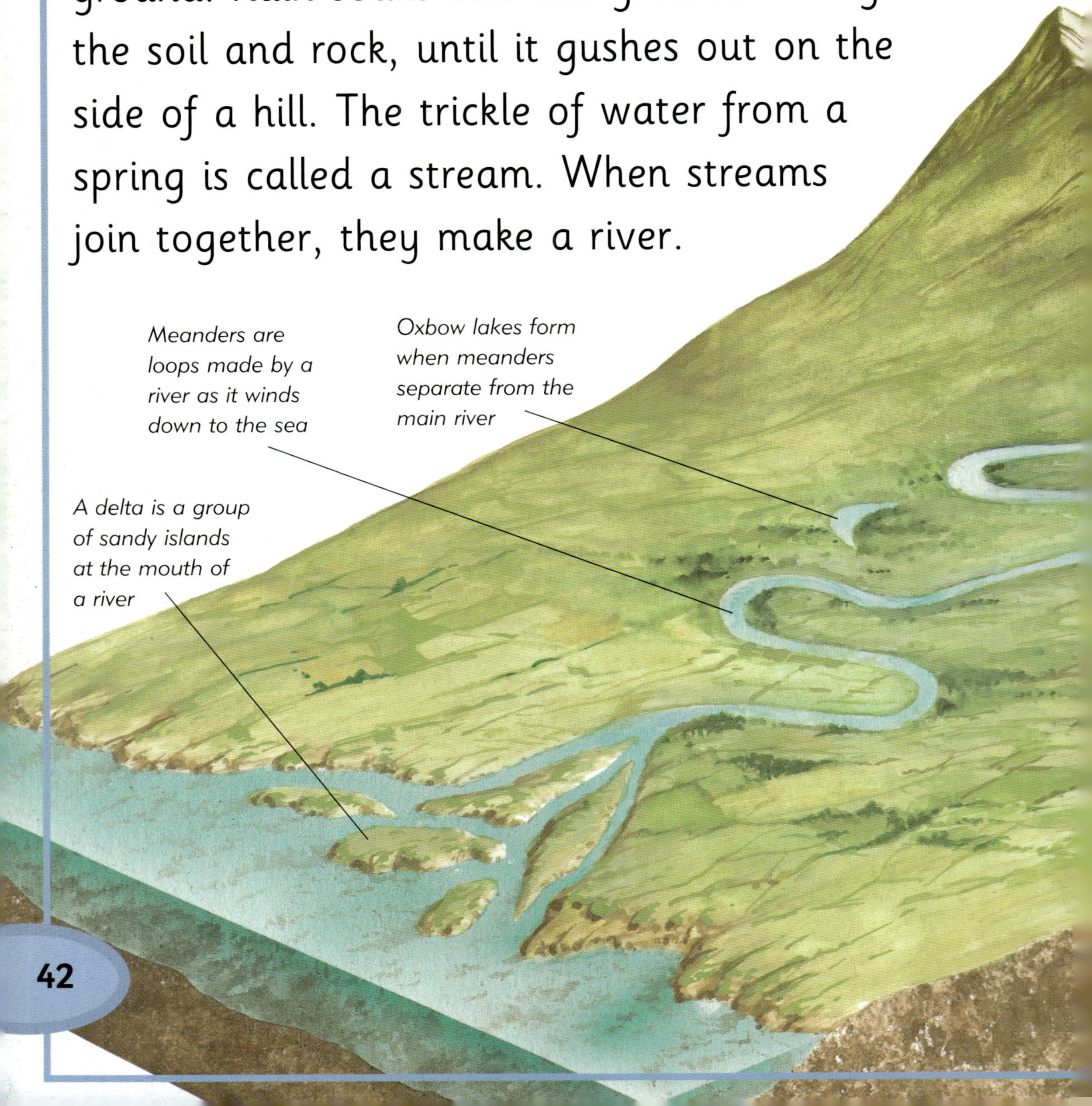

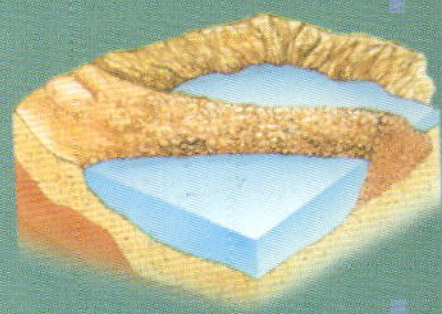

Landslides can fall into rivers and block the flow of water to form lakes.

Lakes can form inside a crater.

Harry's fun facts!

Most lakes are just blue, but some are green, pink, red or even white! The colours are made by tiny creatures called algae or by minerals in the water.

Water, water everywhere

Oceans cover over two-thirds of the Earth's rocky surface. Their total area is about 362 million square kilometres, which means there is more than twice as much ocean as land!

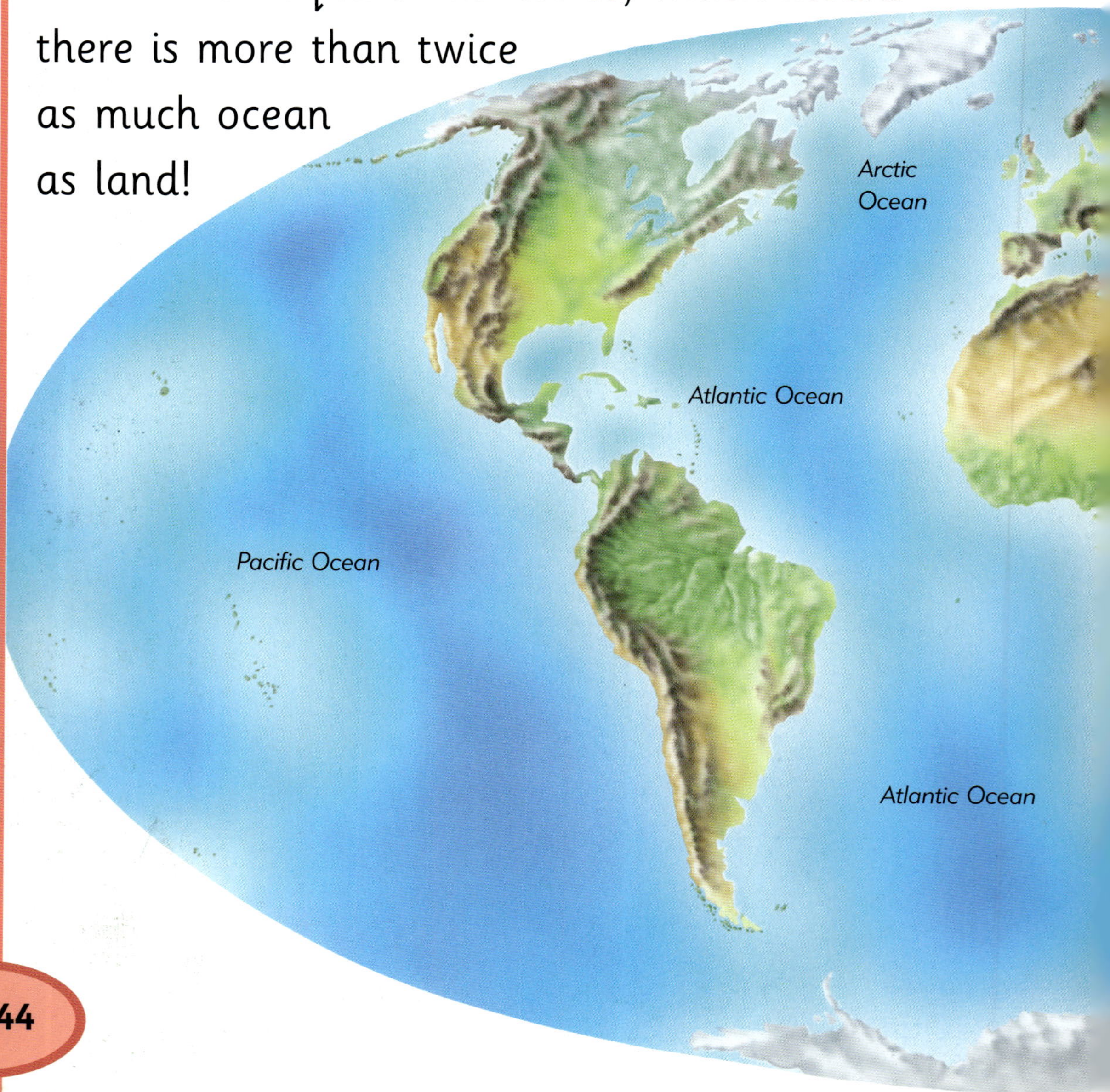

▼ *Although all the oceans flow into each other, we know them as four different oceans – the Pacific, Atlantic, Indian and Arctic. Each ocean is made up of smaller bodies of water called seas.*

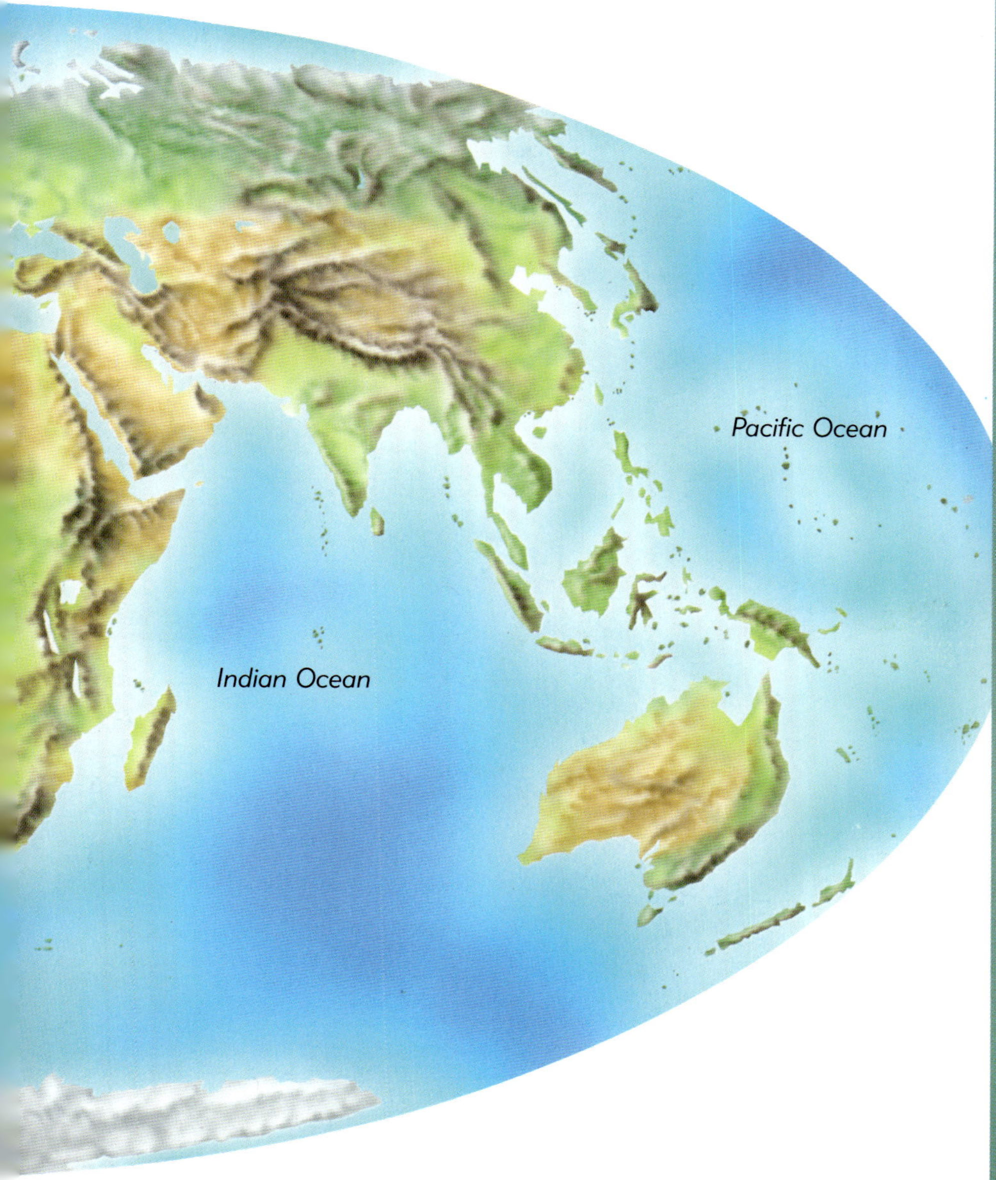

In its deepest parts, *the Pacific Ocean would cover the top of Mount Everest.*

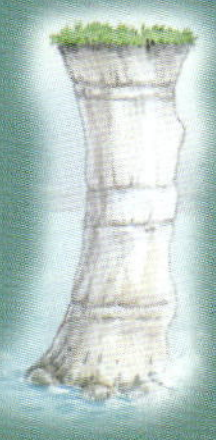

Waves on the surface *of the ocean can carve into rocks creating shapes such as this sea stack.*

Icebergs *break off from huge glaciers and then drift and melt into the oceans.*

Under the ocean

There are plains, mountains and valleys under the ocean, in areas called basins. Each basin has a rim (the flat continental shelf that meets the shore) and sides (the continental slope that drops away from the shelf). The ocean floor moves and its features are changing all the time.

▶ *New islands are born all the time. When an underwater volcano erupts, its lava cools in the water. Layers of lava build up and the volcano grows in size until it peeps above the waves.*

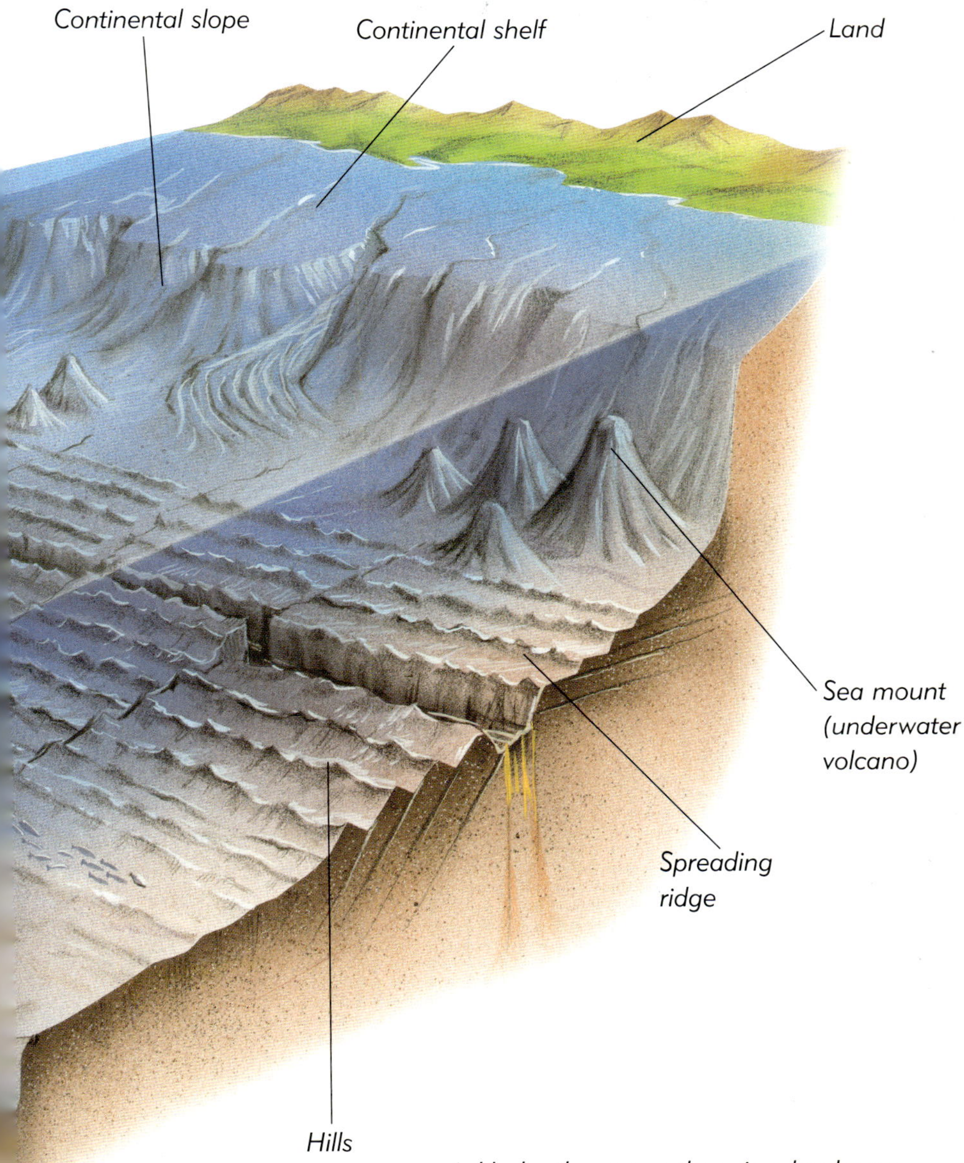

▲ *Under the ocean there is a landscape similar to that found on land. There are flat plains, steep hills, huge underwater volcanoes and deep valleys.*

Stage 1
A coral reef may build up around a volcanic island.

Stage 2
The volcanic island sinks leaving a lagoon (water separate from the open ocean).

Stage 3
An atoll is the ring-shaped coral reef that is left behind and surrounds the lagoon.

Rock pool life

Rock pools are full of all kinds of creatures. Limpets, sponges and anemones all attach themselves to rocks, stopping the waves washing them away. They eat scraps of food washed in with the tide. These pools are also the perfect place for crabs to find food and to hide.

Find the creature!

Unscramble these words to find the names of four different sea creatures:

***1.** PETLIM* ***2.** NGEOPS*

***3.** MONEENA* ***4.** MITREH*

***1.** LIMPET* ***2.** SPONGE* ***3.** ANEMONE* ***4.** HERMIT*

▼ As the tide goes out, water gets trapped amongst the rocks, forming pools. These pools are home to a large variety of animal life.

Anemones are named after flowers, due to their arms that look like petals.

Hermit crabs have no shell, so they use one left behind by another sea creature.

Starfish may lose one of their arms if attacked, but they can grow new ones.

Tropical life

Tiny animals build huge underwater walls. The walls are built up from coral – the leftover skeletons of sea creatures called polyps. Over millions of years, enough skeletons pile up to form huge, wall-like structures called reefs. Coral reefs are full of all sorts of amazing, colourful sea life.

Test your memory!

1. *In its deepest parts, which ocean would cover the top of Mount Everest?*

2. *Which animal uses a shell from another sea creature in which to live?*

3. *What is a ring-shaped coral reef called?*

4. *Name the world's four main oceans.*

1. *Pacific Ocean* **2.** *hermit crab*
3. *an atoll*
4. *Pacific, Atlantic, Indian and Arctic*

Cleaner wrasse *fish nibble bits of dirt off bigger fishes' bodies.*

Stone fish *rest on the seabed and look exactly like stones!*

Clownfish *swim unharmed amongst sea anemones' tentacles.*

▲ *Most fish found in coral reefs have colourful spots or stripes. This helps them to blend with their surroundings, making it hard for a hunter to spot them.*

Our atmosphere

Our planet is wrapped in a blanket of air. We call this blanket the atmosphere. It stretches hundreds of kilometres above our heads. The blanket keeps in heat, especially at night when part of the planet faces away from the Sun. During the day, the blanket becomes a sunscreen instead. Without an atmosphere, there would be no weather.

◀ *The Earth is surrounded by the atmosphere. It acts as a blanket, protecting us from the Sun's fierce rays.*

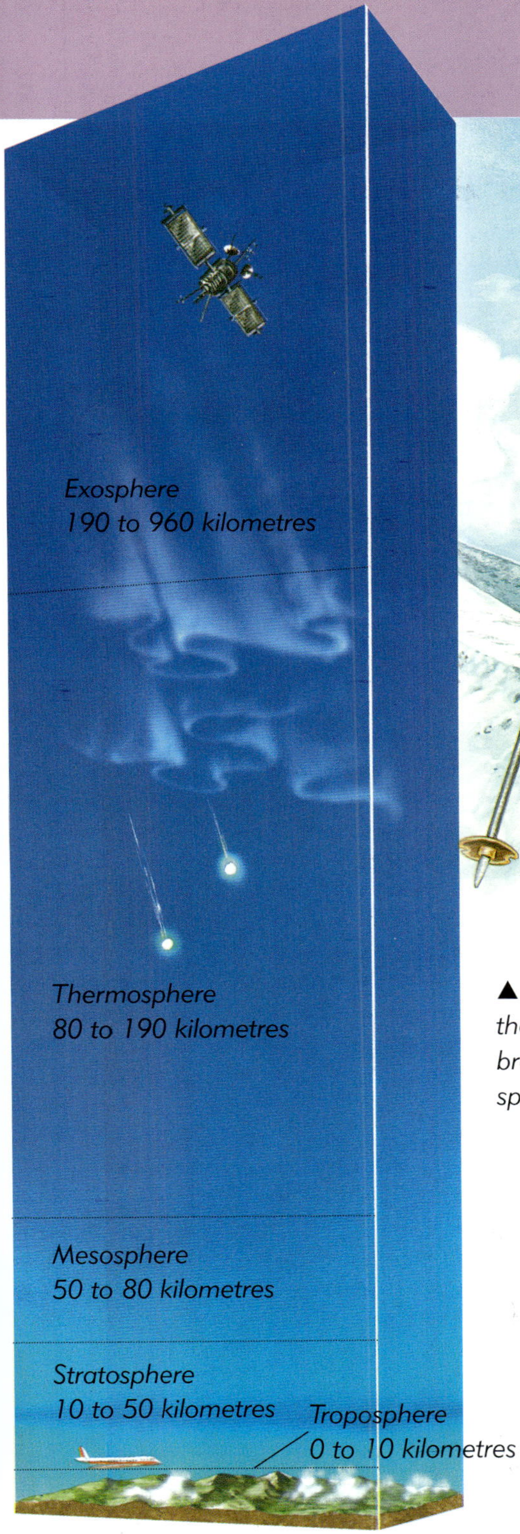

▲ *The higher up you go, the less oxygen there is in the air. We need oxygen to breathe, so mountaineers often wear special breathing equipment.*

◀ *The atmosphere stretches right into space. Scientists have split it into five layers, or spheres, such as the troposphere.*

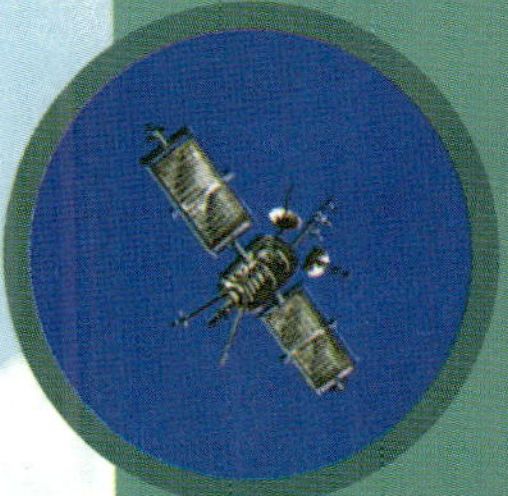

Low-level satellites *orbit within the outer layers of the atmosphere.*

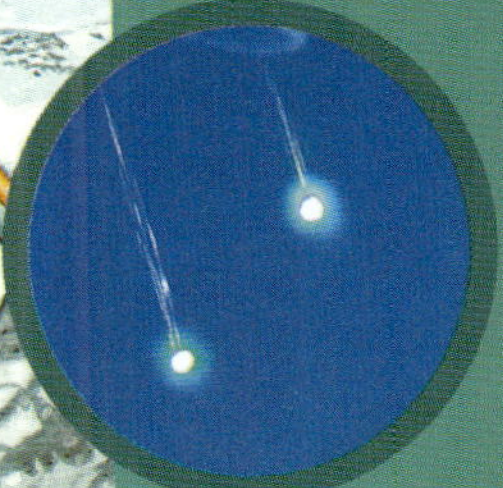

Meteorites, *pieces of rock from space, burn up in the atmosphere.*

Mountaineers *wear masks that help them breathe in more oxygen.*

What is weather?

Rain, sunshine, snow and storms are all types of weather. Weather affects how we live, and how animals and plants survive. Different types of weather are caused by what is happening in the atmosphere, the air above our heads. In parts of the world, the weather changes daily, in others, it is nearly always the same.

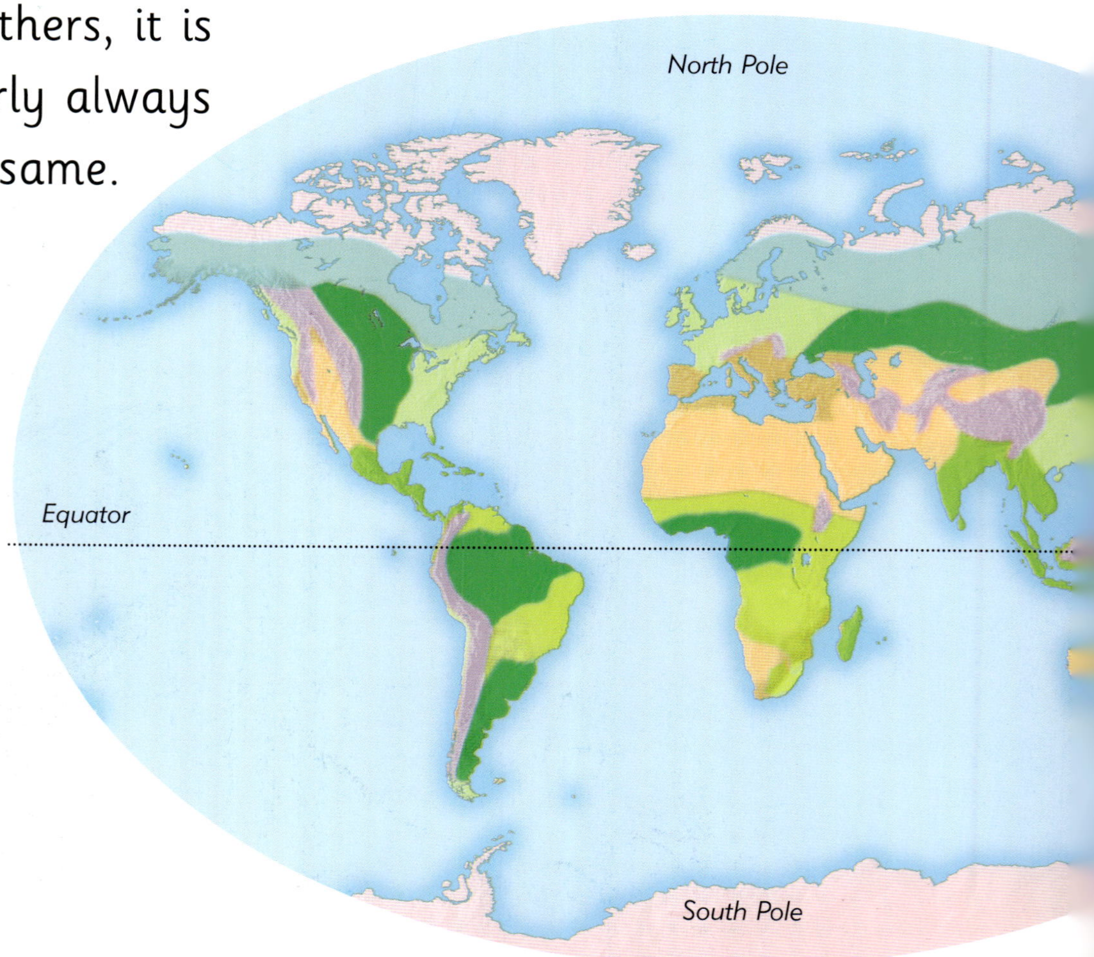

▼ *Use the coloured rings around the pictures below to match the different climate scenes to the main map.*

Tropical forest

Tropical grassland

Cold temperate

Temperate grassland

Desert

Wet temperate

Mountainous

Polar

Dry temperate

Most of the world *has a temperate climate – it is neither too hot nor too cold.*

Near the North *and South Poles, there is a cold, polar climate.*

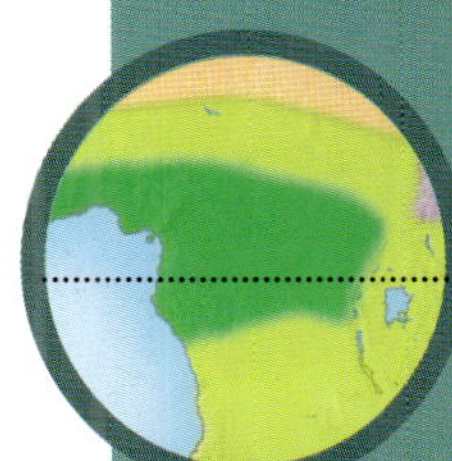

The Equator *is an imaginary line around the middle of the Earth.*

All the seasons

The reason for the seasons lies in space. Our planet Earth plots a path through space that takes it around the Sun. This path, or orbit, takes one year. The Earth is tilted, so over the year first one and then the other Pole leans towards the Sun, giving us seasons.

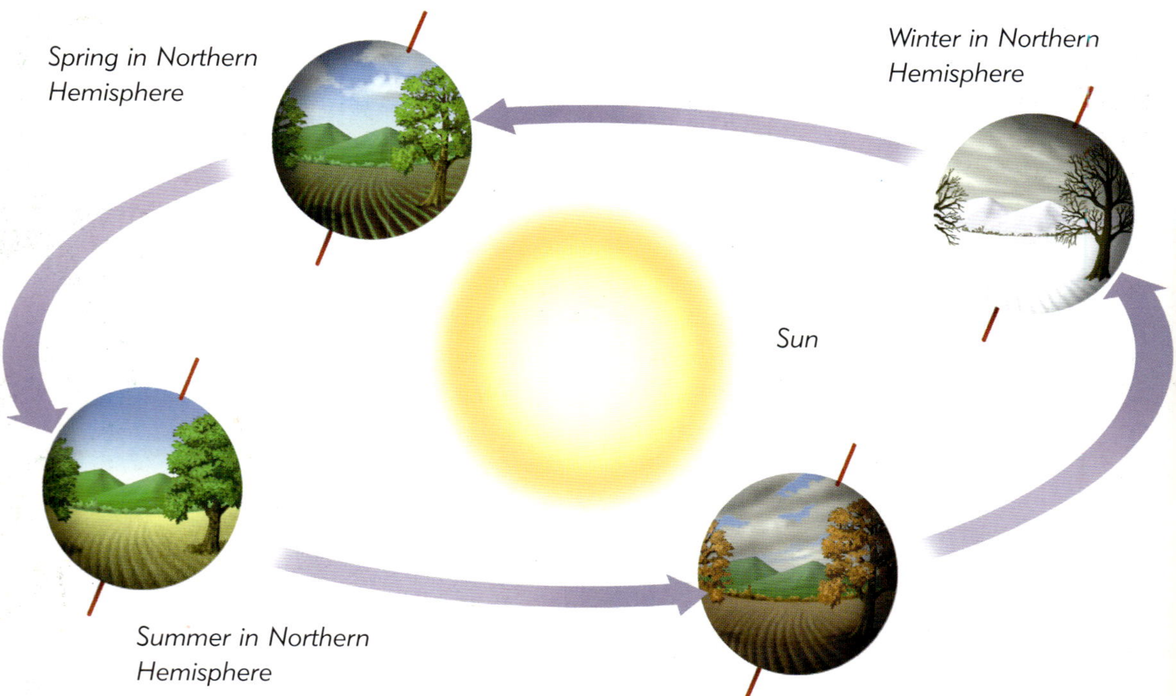

▲ *In June in the Northern Hemisphere, the North Pole leans towards the Sun. The Sun heats the northern half of the Earth and there is summer.*

▲ At the North Pole during the height of summer, the Sun never disappears below the horizon.

Summer *in the Northern Hemisphere is between June and September.*

Winter *in the Northern Hemisphere is between December and March.*

▼ *Many forests change colour in autumn. Trees prepare for the winter months ahead by losing their leaves. First, though, they suck back the precious green chlorophyll, or dye, in their leaves. This makes them turn glorious golden colours.*

Sidney's fun facts!

In Stockholm, Sweden, the longest day lasts 21 hours because the Sun disappears below the horizon for only three hours!

Tropical seasons

Many parts of the tropics have two seasons, not four. The tropics are the parts of the world closest to the Equator. In June, tropical areas north of the Equator have the strongest heat and heaviest rains. In December, it is the turn of the areas south of the Equator.

◀ *Rainforests have rainy weather all year round – but there is still a wet and dry season. It is just that the wet season is even wetter!*

▼ *Monsoons are winds that carry heavy rains. The rains fall in the tropics during the hot, rainy season. They can cause chaos, turning streets to rivers and even washing people's homes away.*

Daily rainfall *feeds the lush rainforest vegetation.*

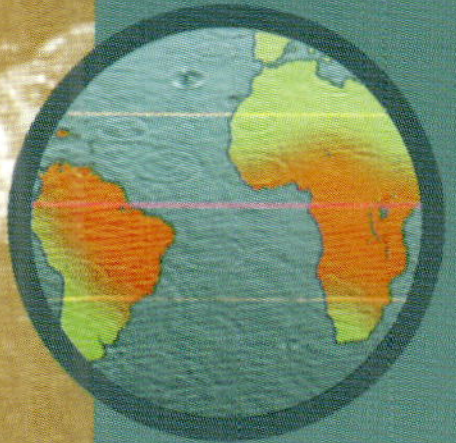

The tropics *are always hot, as they are constantly facing the Sun.*

▼ *The tropics (shown here in red) lie either side of the Equator, between lines of latitude called the Tropic of Cancer and the Tropic of Capricorn.*

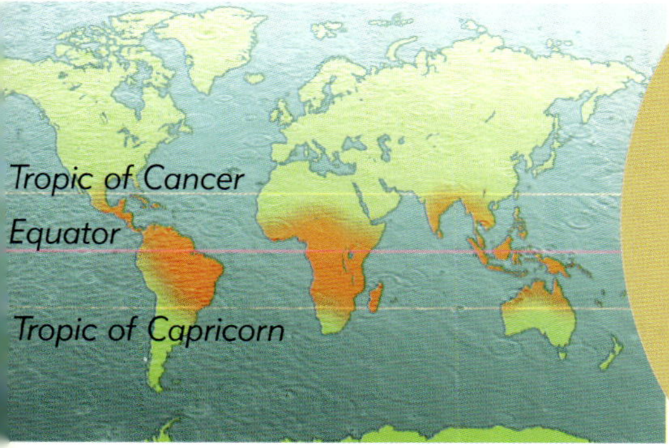

Sidney's fun facts!

In parts of monsoon India, over 26,000 millimetres of rain have fallen in a single year!

Scorching Sun

All our heat comes from the Sun. The Sun is a star, a super-hot ball of burning gases. It gives off heat rays that travel 150 million kilometres through space to our planet. Over the journey, the rays cool down, but they can still scorch the Earth.

▶ *The Sahara Desert is the sunniest place on Earth. It is home to people such as the Tuareg Arabs.*

Test your memory!

1. *How many seasons are there in the tropics?*

2. *What is the name of the imaginary line that runs around the middle of the Earth?*

3. *What kind of climate will you find in the North Pole?*

1. *two* ***2.*** *the Equator* ***3.*** *a cold, polar climate*

▶ *Too much sun brings drought. Without rain, crops die and people and their animals go hungry.*

Desert peoples *cover their heads to protect them from the hot sun and sand.*

Camels *have long eyelashes to keep sand out of their eyes.*

Strong winds *blow the dry earth causing dust storms.*

Thunderclap!

Thunderstorms are most likely in summer. Hot weather creates warm, moist air that rises and forms tall cumulonimbus clouds. Inside each cloud, water droplets and ice crystals bang about, building up positive and negative electrical charges. Electricity flows between the charges, creating a flash that heats the air around it – this is lightning.

How close?

Lightning and thunder happen at the same time, but light travels faster than sound. Count the seconds between the flash and the clap and divide them by three. This is how many kilometres away the storm is.

Lightning that travels from the cloud to the ground is called fork lightning.

▲ Lightning comes in different colours. If there is rain in the thundercloud, the lightning looks red. If there is hail, it looks blue.

◀ Lightning is so hot that it makes the air expand (spread out), making a loud noise or thunderclap.

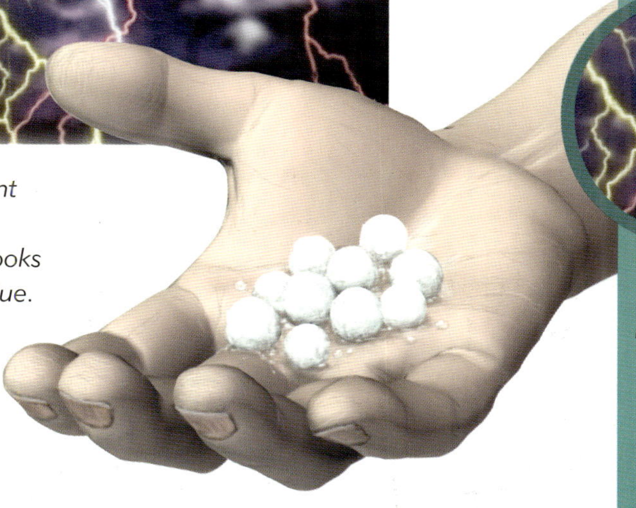

▼ Hailstones are chunks of ice that fall from thunderclouds.

Hailstones can be bigger than melons!

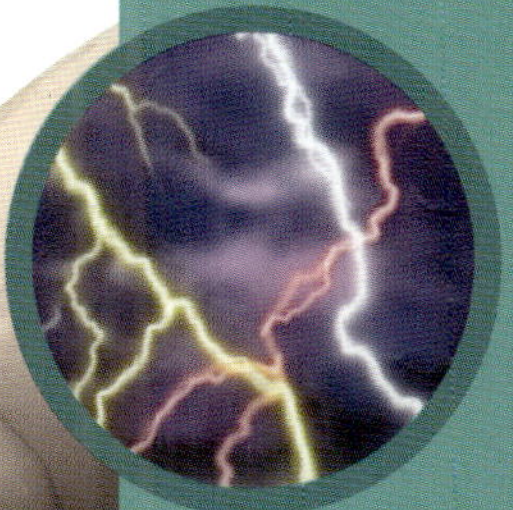

Dramatic flashes of lightning light up the sky.

In a spin!

Tornadoes spin at speeds of 480 kilometres an hour! These whirling columns of wind are some of the most destructive storms on Earth. They form in strong thunderstorms, when the back part of the thundercloud starts spinning. The spinning air forms a funnel that reaches down towards the Earth. When it touches the ground, it becomes a tornado.

▶ *A tornado can cause great damage to anything in its path.*

▲ *Hundreds of tornadoes happen in Tornado Alley, in the American Mid-West, shown in the shaded area.*

Waterspouts *are pillars of spinning water sucked up by a tornado.*

Dust devils *are desert tornadoes that create a whirling storm of sand.*

Sidney's fun facts!

Waterspouts can suck up fish living in a lake!

Our world of science

Why do we need science? Even one hundred books like this could not explain all the reasons. Toasters, bicycles, mobile phones, computers, cars, light bulbs – all the gadgets and machines we use every day are the results of scientific discoveries.

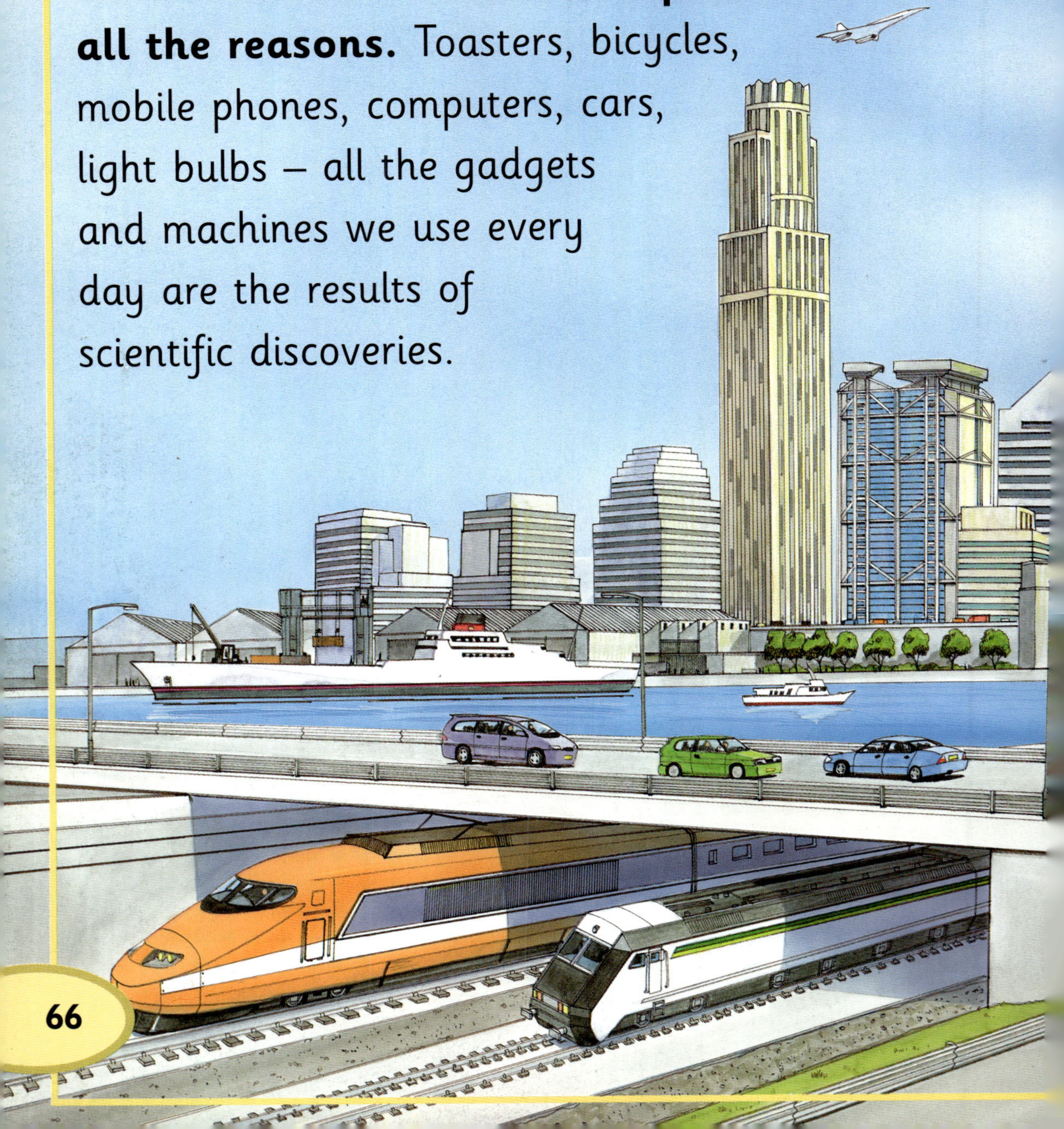

▼ *In a big city, almost every vehicle, building and machine is based on science and technology.*

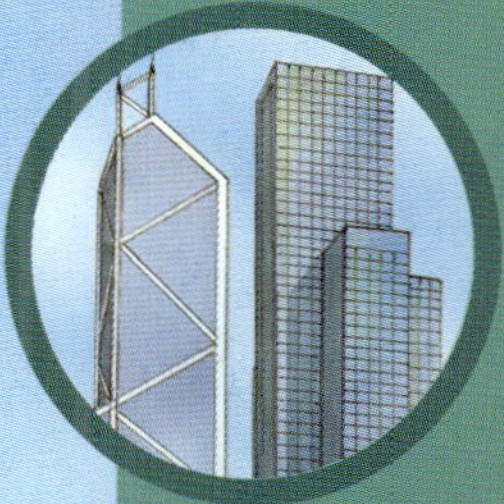

Skyscrapers *are tall buildings that tower in the air.*

Cranes *are used to lift heavy objects.*

Trains *and other transport are built using science.*

Machines are everywhere!

Machines help us do many things, or they make doing them easier. Every time you play on a see-saw, you are using a machine. And where would you be without wheels? Not going very far! Levers, screws, pulleys and wheels are all simple but useful machines.

▲ *The wheel is a circular disc that turns around its centre on a bar called an axle.*

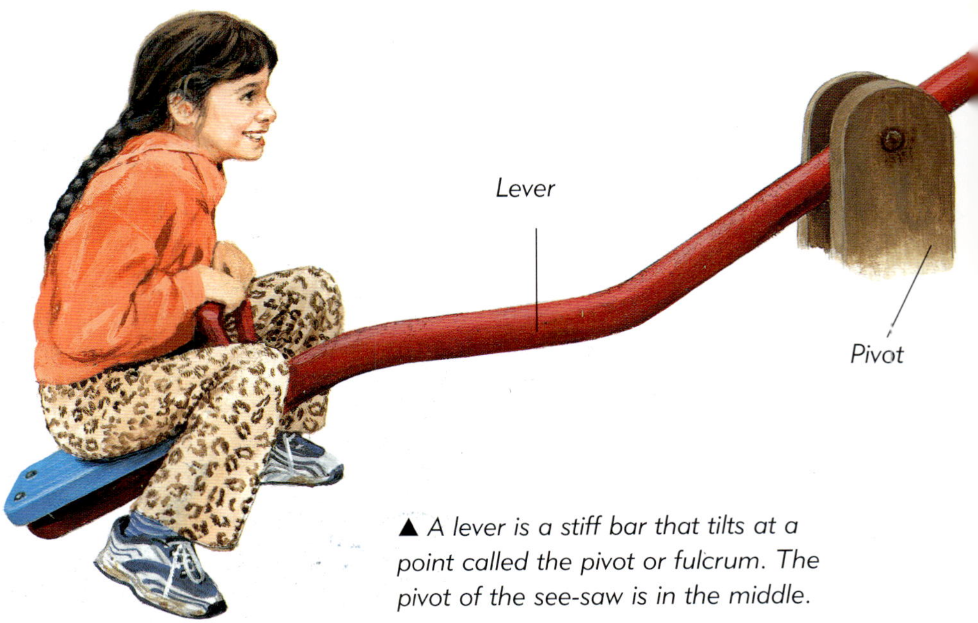

▲ *A lever is a stiff bar that tilts at a point called the pivot or fulcrum. The pivot of the see-saw is in the middle.*

▼ *The screw is a ridge, or thread, wrapped around a bar or pole. It changes a small turning motion into a powerful pulling movement.*

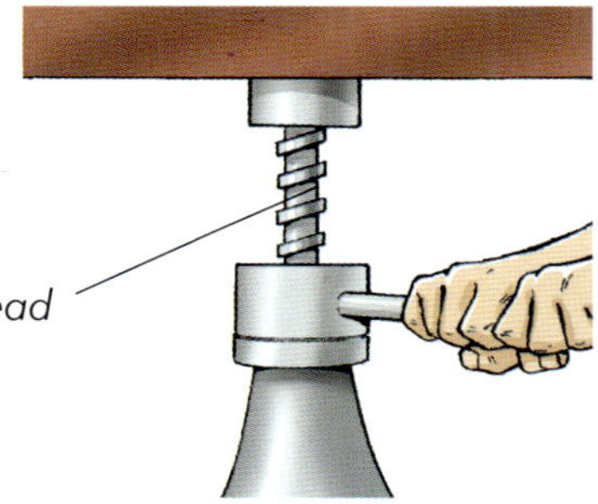

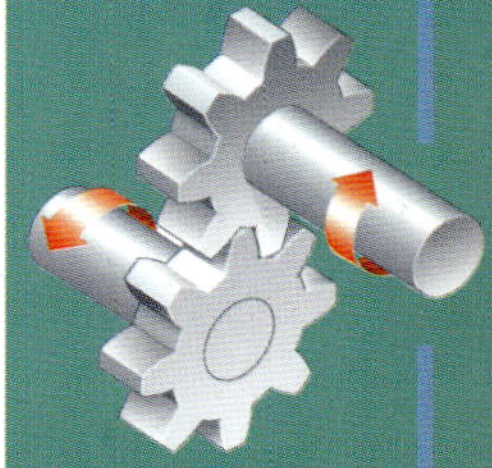

***Gears** can slow down or speed up the turning direction of a force.*

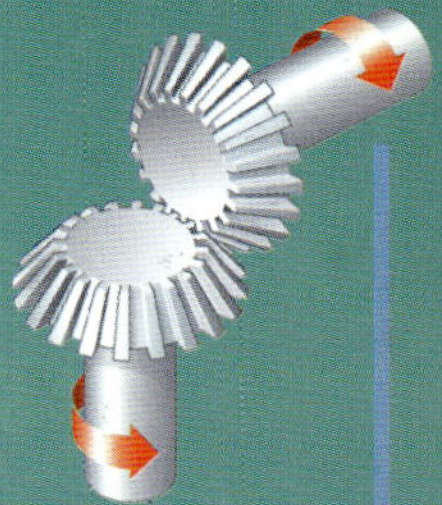

***The wheels** on gears have pointed teeth around the edges.*

▼ *A pulley turns around like a wheel. It has a groove around its edge for a cable or rope.*

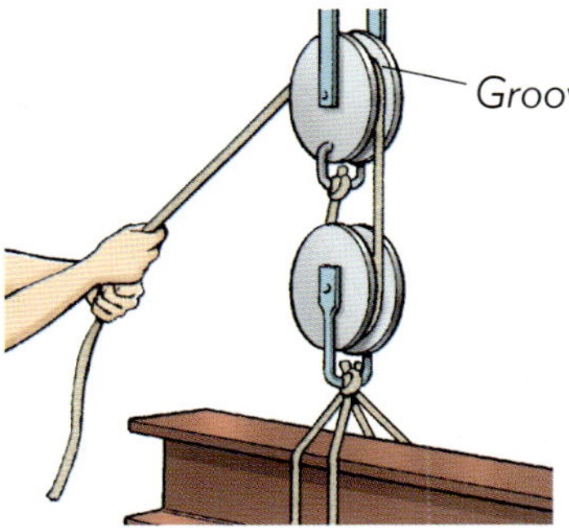

Samuel's fun facts!

A ramp is a simple machine called an inclined plane. It is easier to walk up a ramp than to jump straight to the top.

Hot science

Fire! Flames! Burning! Heat! The science of heat is important in all kinds of ways. Not only do we cook with heat, but we also warm our homes and heat water. Burning happens in all kinds of engines in cars, trucks, planes and rockets. It is also used in factory processes, from making steel to shaping plastics.

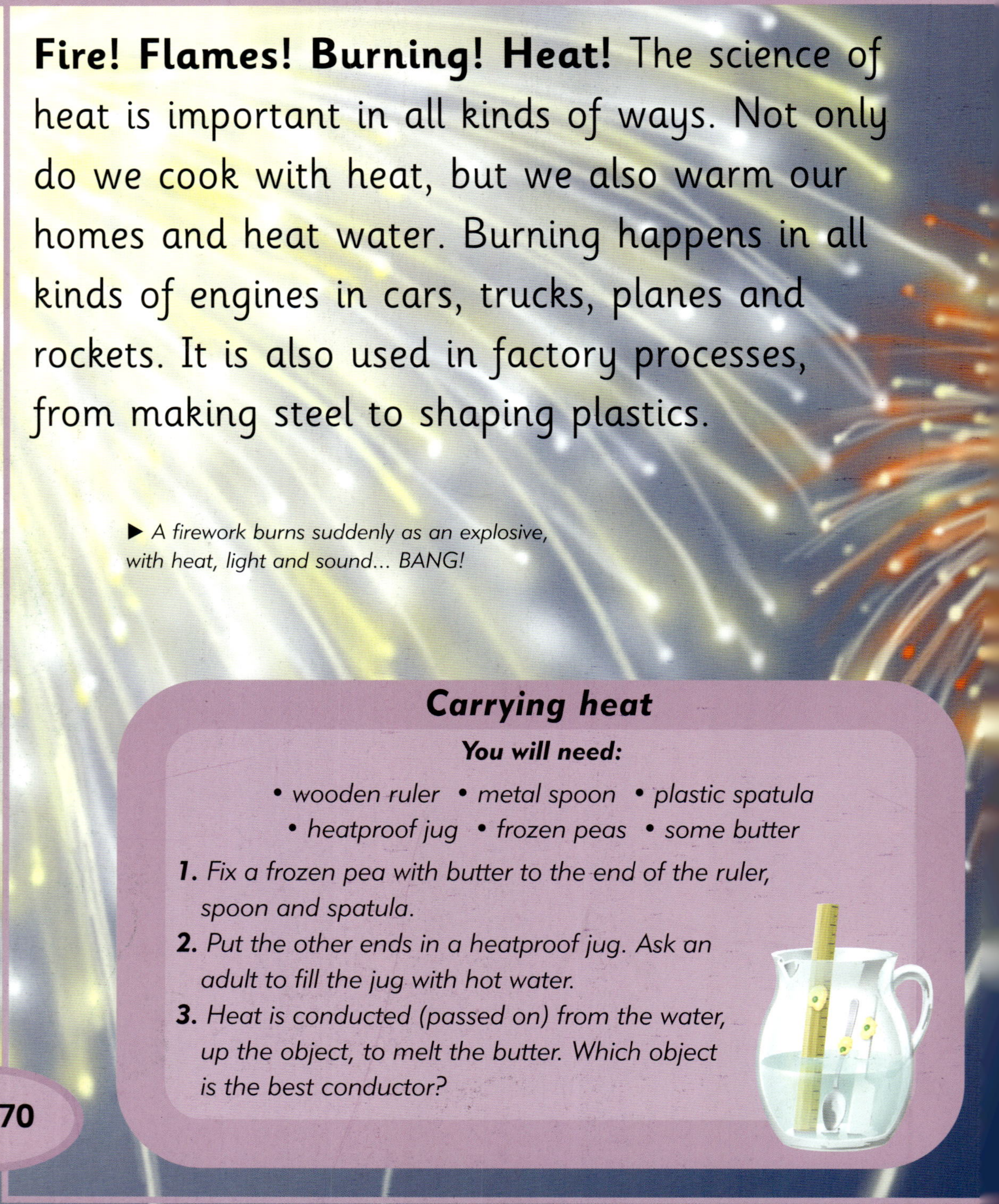

▶ A firework burns suddenly as an explosive, with heat, light and sound... BANG!

Carrying heat

You will need:

• wooden ruler • metal spoon • plastic spatula • heatproof jug • frozen peas • some butter

1. *Fix a frozen pea with butter to the end of the ruler, spoon and spatula.*

2. *Put the other ends in a heatproof jug. Ask an adult to fill the jug with hot water.*

3. *Heat is conducted (passed on) from the water, up the object, to melt the butter. Which object is the best conductor?*

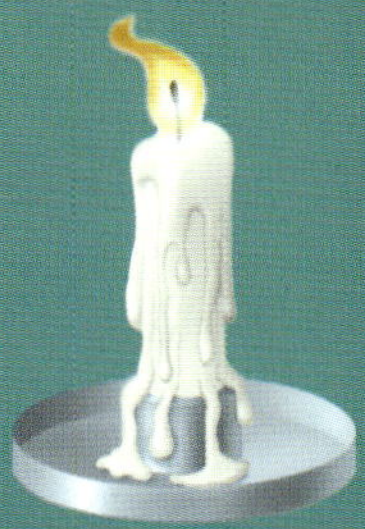

***Hot air** rises from a candle. This movement of heat is called convection.*

***A hot drink** passes its heat to the spoon, warming it up. Heat moves by conduction.*

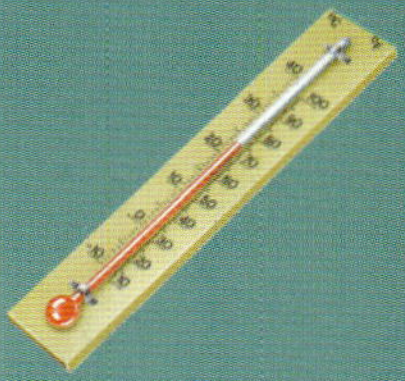

***A thermometer** is used for measuring heat.*

What a noise!

Listening to the radio or television, playing music, shouting at each other – they all depend on the science of sound – acoustics.

Sounds are like invisible waves in the air. These waves travel about 330 metres every second. This is one million times slower than light waves.

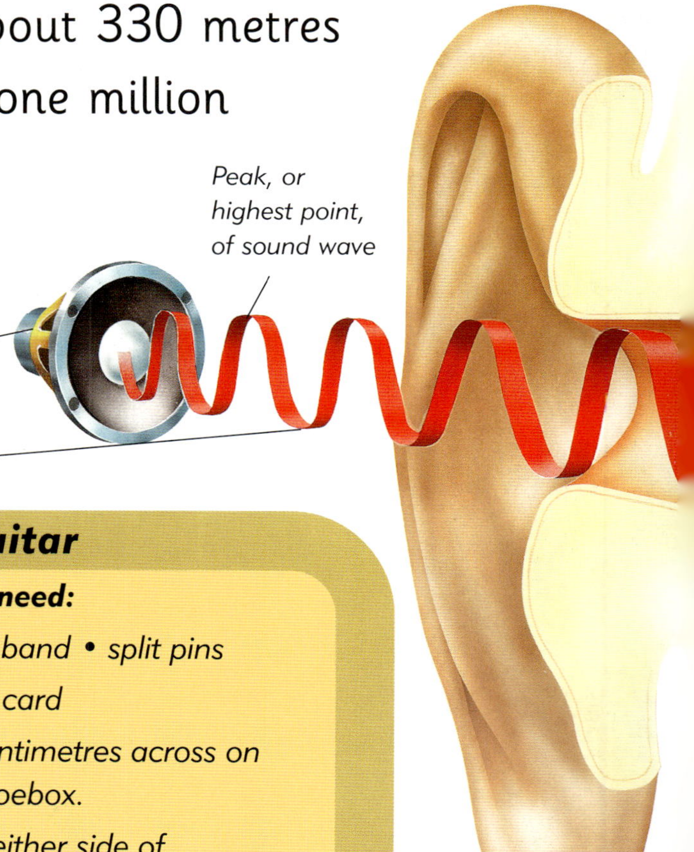

Box guitar

You will need:

• *shoebox* • *elastic band* • *split pins* • *some card*

1. *Cut a hole about ten centimetres across on one side of an empty shoebox.*

2. *Push split pins through either side of the hole, and stretch an elastic band between them.*

3. *Pluck the band. Hear how the air and box vibrate.*

▼ *We cannot see sound waves but we can certainly hear them. They are ripples of high and low pressure in air. Pressure is the force that one object presses onto another.*

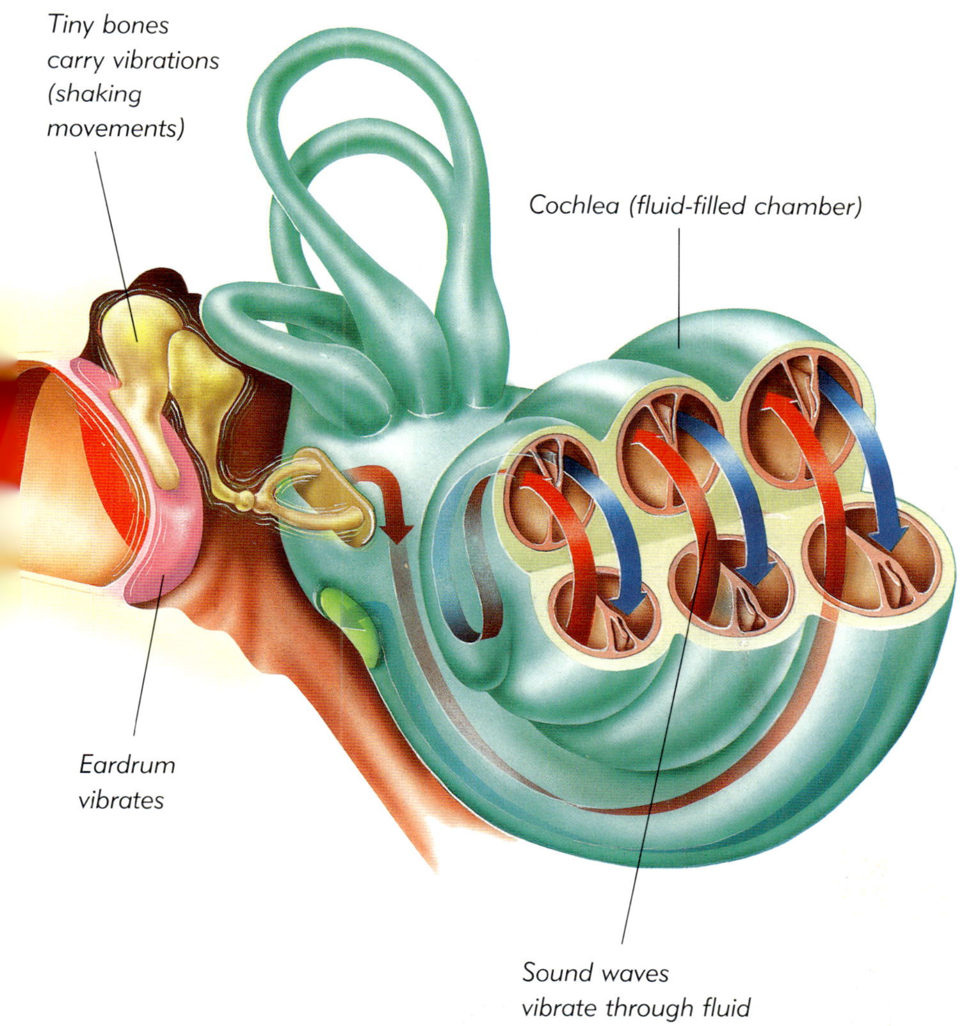

Loudness *is measured in decibels, dB. A quiet sound, such as whispering, is about 20 dB.*

A fast-moving express train *is about 80 dB.*

A jet plane *taking off is 120 dB. Too much noise can damage the ears.*

Light at work

Almost everything you do relies on light and the science of light, which is called optics.

Light is a form of energy that you can see. Light waves are made of electricity and magnetism – and they are tiny. About 2000 of them laid end to end would stretch across this full stop.

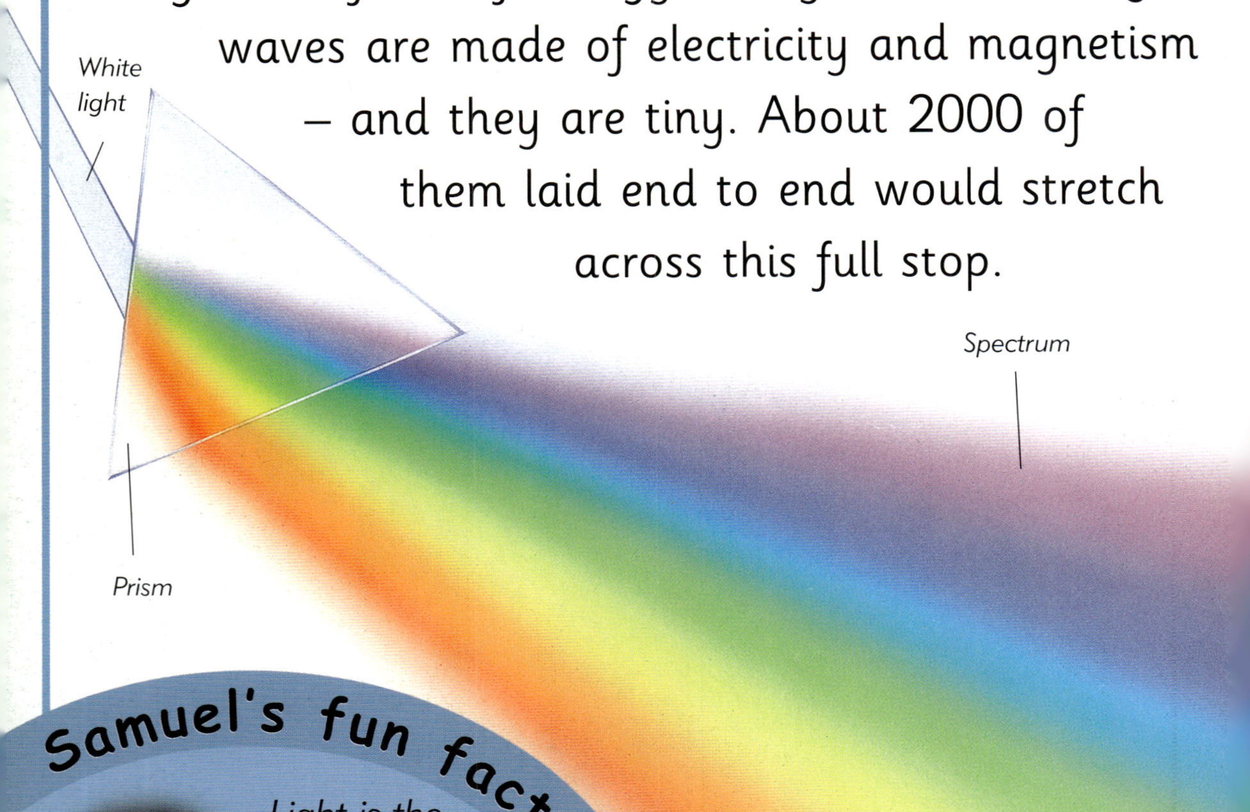

▲ *When white light passes through a prism (a triangular piece of glass), it splits into seven colours. These colours are called the spectrum.*

Samuel's fun facts!

Light is the fastest thing in the Universe. It travels through space at 300,000 kilometres a second.

▼ *Light waves bounce off surfaces which are smooth, such as a mirror. This is called reflection.*

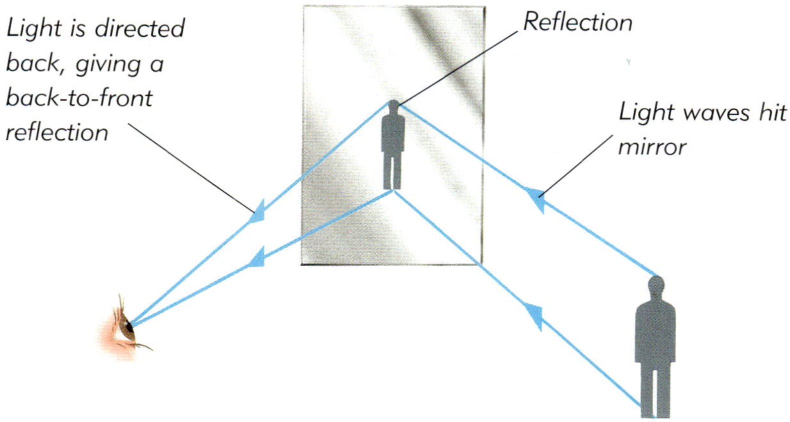

▼ *A lens is a curved piece of glass or plastic that bends light to make things look bigger or smaller.*

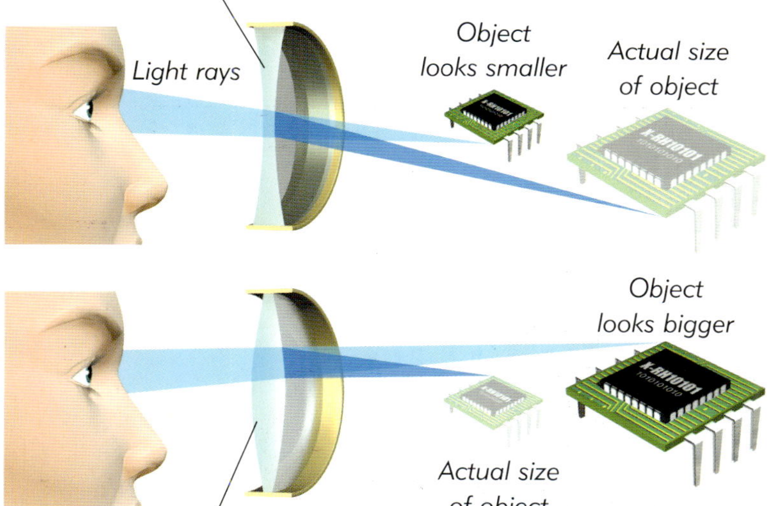

Ordinary light from the Sun is called white light.

Glass and water bend, or refract light, making a straw look bent in the glass.

Cameras make pictures by using lenses and light.

What is electricity?

Electricity is our favourite form of energy. Imagine no washing machine, no electric light and no vacuum cleaner! We send it along wires and plug hundreds of machines into it. Electricity depends on electrons, tiny parts of atoms.

▼ When electrons are 'pushed', they hop from one atom to the next. This is how electricity flows.

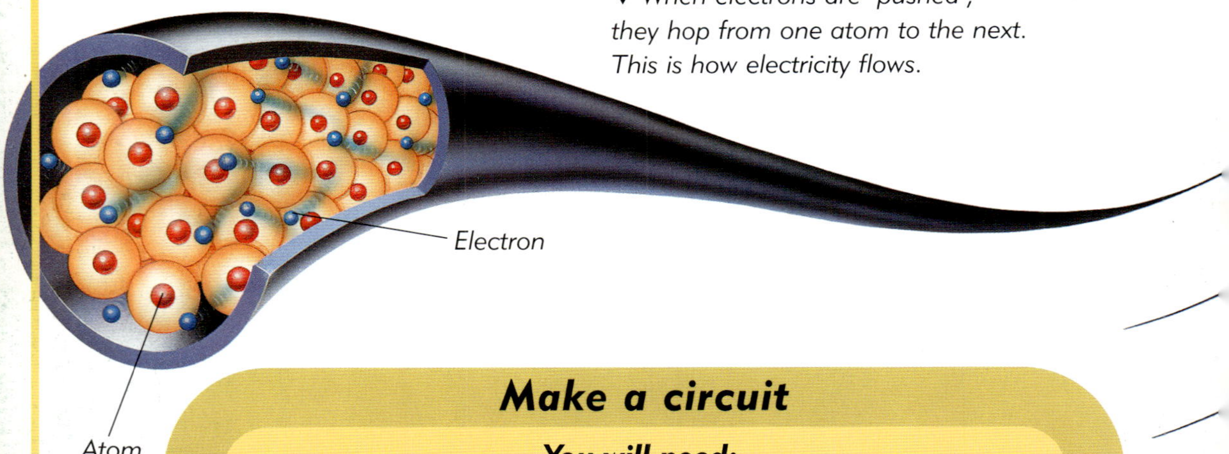

Make a circuit

You will need:

- *lightbulb* • *3-volt battery* • *some wire*
- *plastic ruler* • *metal spoon* • *some dry card*

1. *Ask an adult to help. Join a bulb to a battery with pieces of wire, as shown. Electricity flows round the circuit (loop) and lights the bulb.*
2. *Make a gap in the circuit and put the other objects into it, to see if they allow electricity to flow again.*

▼ *A power station makes enough electricity for thousands of homes.*

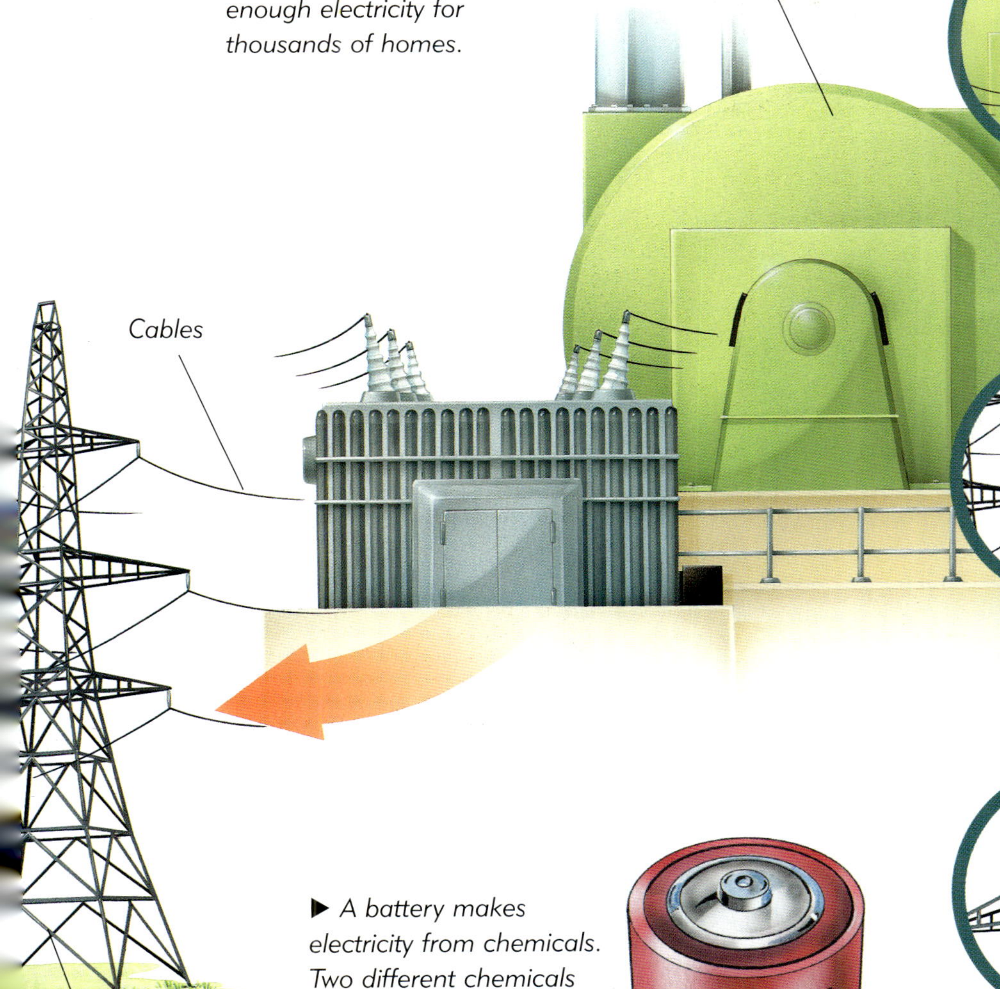

The generator *gives the 'push' that starts the electrons flowing.*

Cables *carry electricity at thousands of volts.*

Pylons *hold cables safe above the ground.*

▶ *A battery makes electricity from chemicals. Two different chemicals next to each other, such as an acid and a metal, swap electrons and get the electricity flowing.*

Invisible waves

The air is full of waves we cannot see or hear, unless we have the right machine. Radio waves are a form of electrical and magnetic energy, just like heat and light waves, microwaves and X-rays. They all travel at an equal speed – the speed of light.

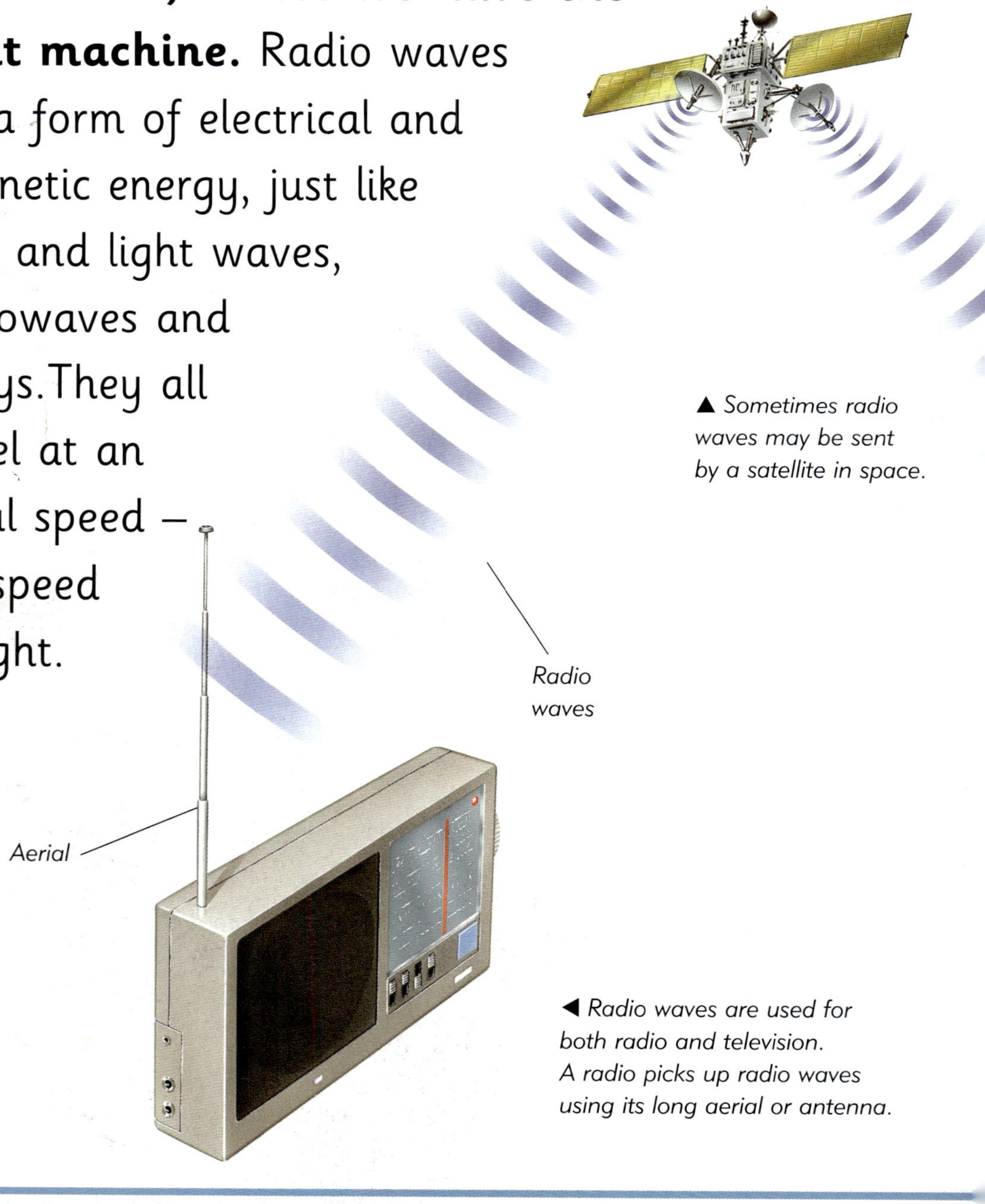

▲ *Sometimes radio waves may be sent by a satellite in space.*

◀ *Radio waves are used for both radio and television. A radio picks up radio waves using its long aerial or antenna.*

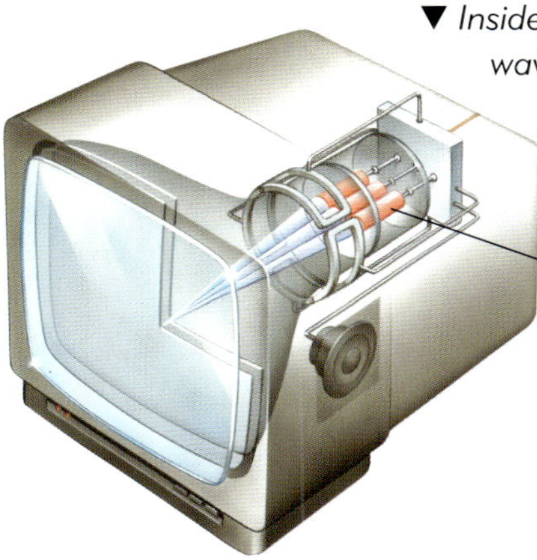

▼ *Inside a TV set, the pattern of radio waves is changed to electrical signals. These make the pictures and sounds.*

▲ *A TV screen is coated with tiny coloured dots inside. When electrons hit the dots, they glow and make the picture.*

▲ *A satellite dish picks up radio waves for TV channels.*

***Radio waves** travel vast distances.*

***Three colours of dots** join to make up the other colours on a TV screen.*

Samuel's fun facts!

Radio waves travel easily though space, but they hardly pass at all through water.

Computer science

Computers are amazing machines. They have to be told exactly what to do, so we put in instructions and information, by various means. These include typing on a keyboard, inserting a disc, using a joystick, or linking up a camera, scanner or another computer.

Compu-scramble!

Unscramble these words to find the names of four different computer parts:

1. *USEOM* ***2.*** *TONMIOR*
3. *CRIOMPICH* ***4.*** *BEYKROAD*

1. *MOUSE* ***2.*** *MONITOR* ***3.*** *MICROCHIP*
4. *KEYBOARD*

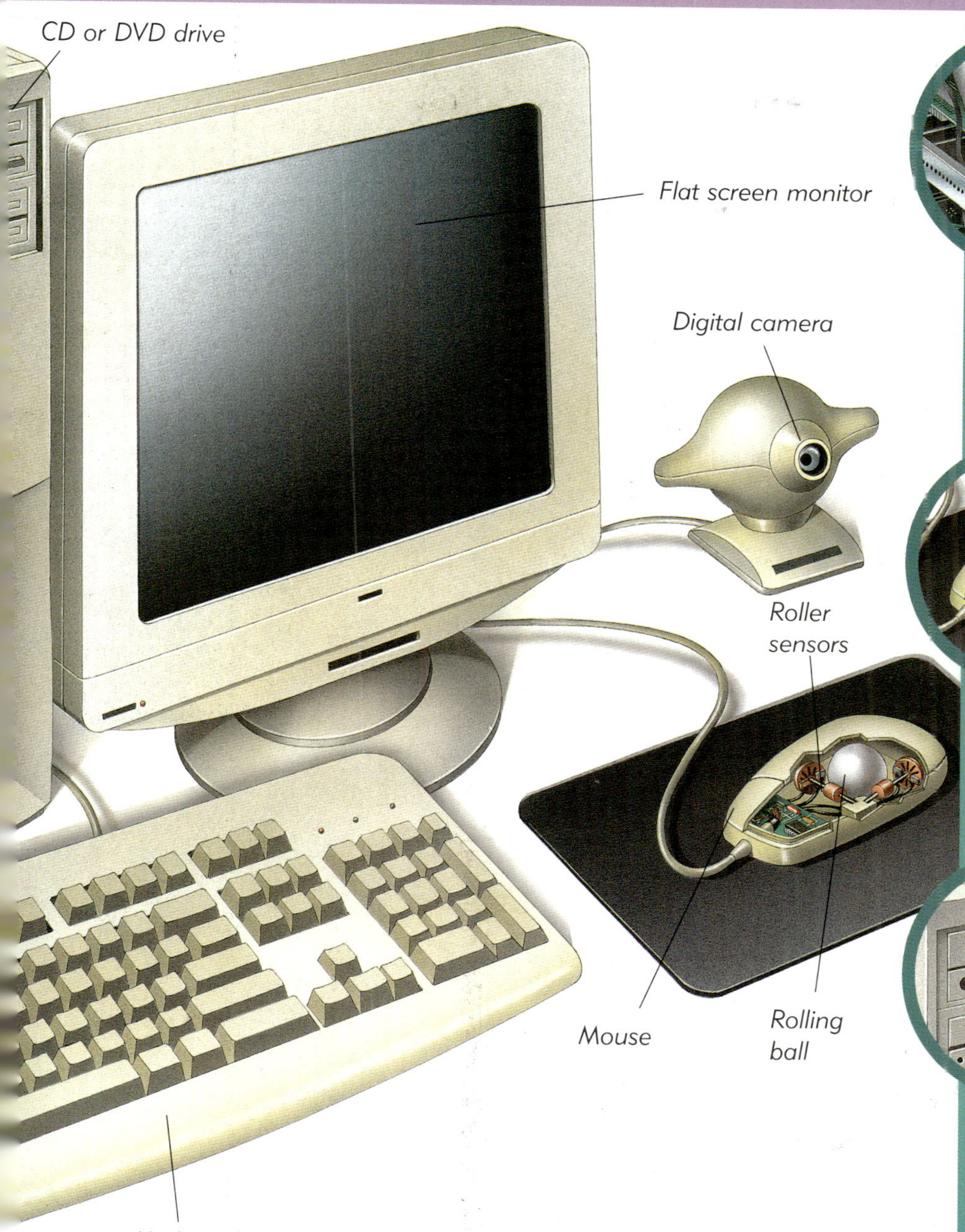

▲ This is a PC, or personal computer. Most computers are controlled by instructions from a keyboard and a mouse.

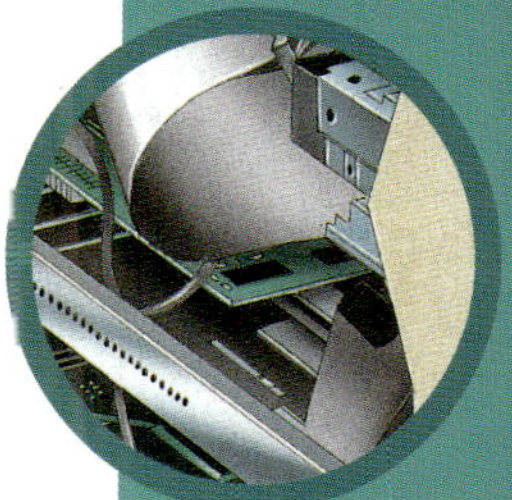

Microchips *are the main 'brain' of a computer.*

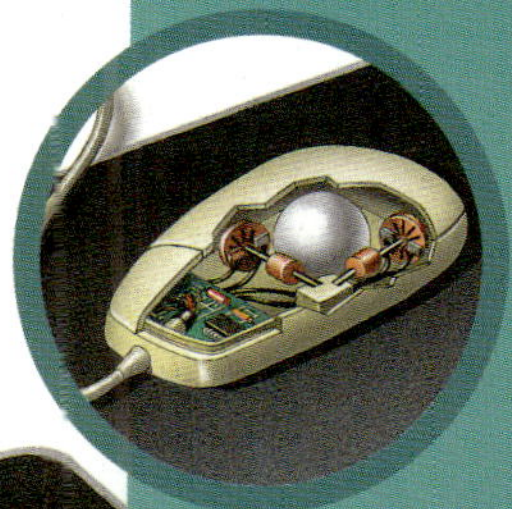

The mouse *moves a pointer around the screen.*

The disc drive *stores information on CD or DVD.*

Amazing web

The world is at your fingertips – if you are on the Internet. The 'Net' is one of the most amazing results of modern-day science. It is a worldwide network of computers, linked like one huge electrical spider's web.

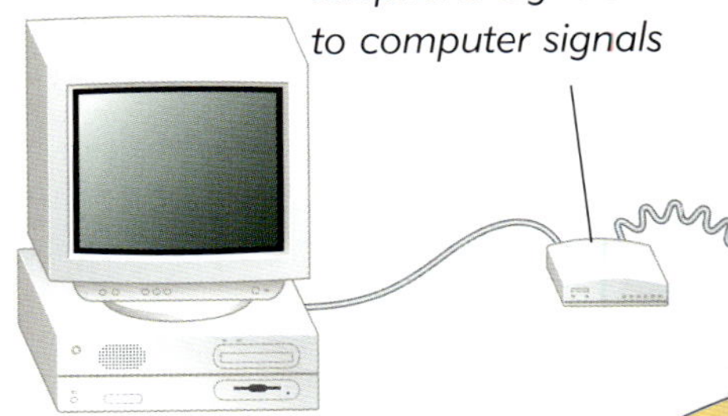

A modem changes telephone signals to computer signals

Email is a quick way of sending messages to other Internet users

◀ *Mobile phones can connect to the Internet using their radio link.*

▲ *The web spans the world as signals of electricity, radio, light and microwaves.*

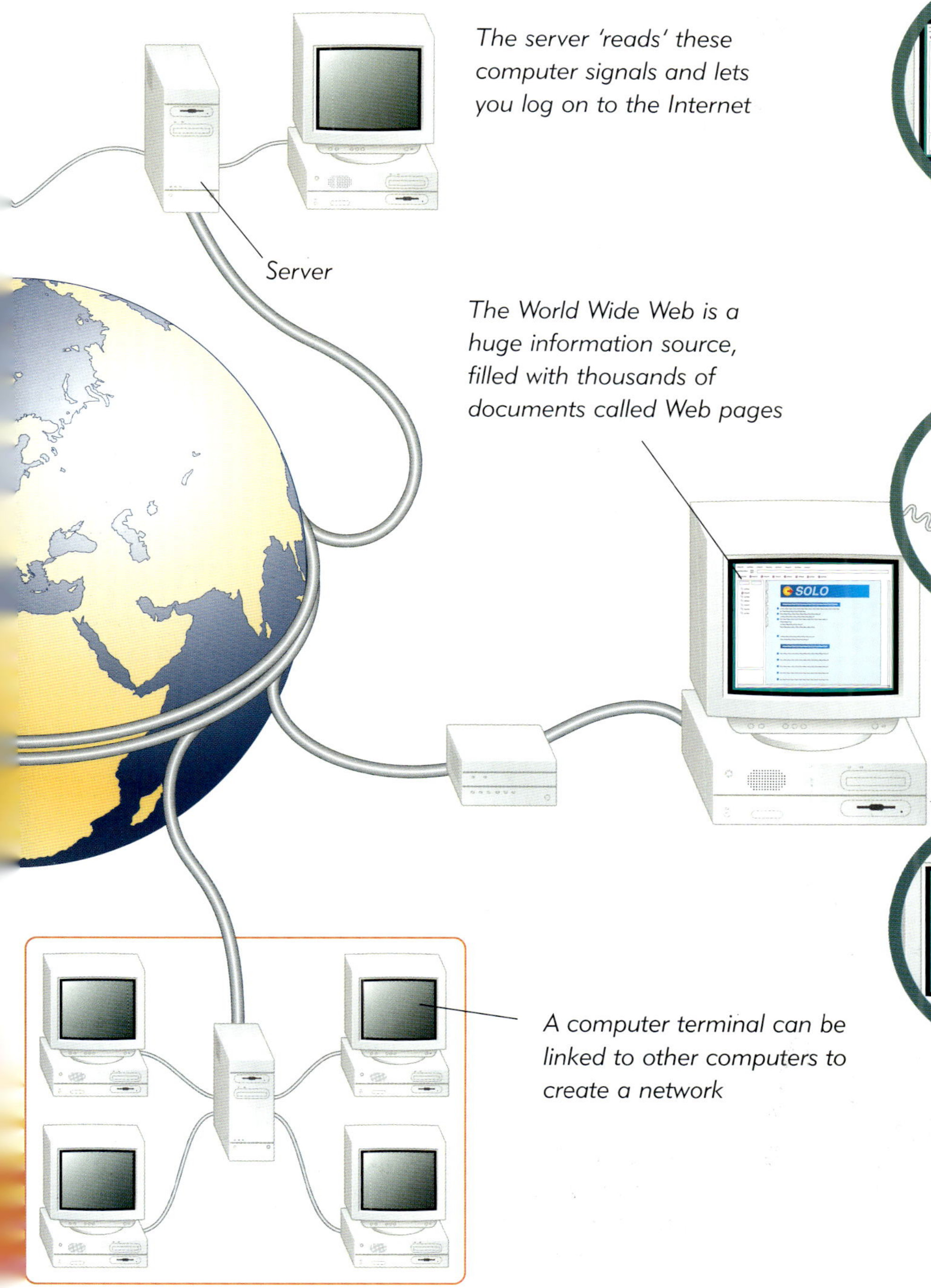

A website *is like a leaflet, book or video of information.*

Telephone wires *carry signals from computer to computer.*

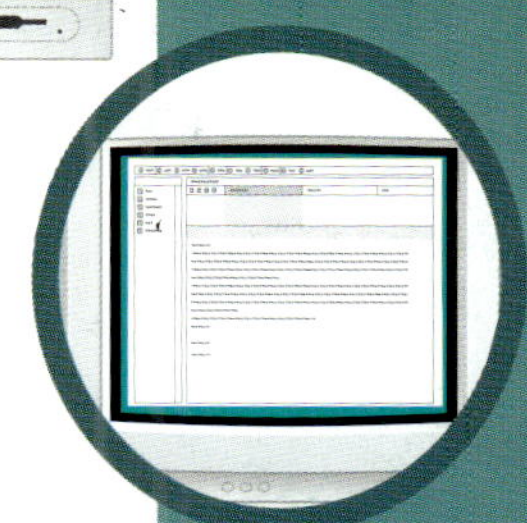

Email *stands for electronic mail.*

Watching the weather

Satellites help save lives. Their bird's-eye view of the Earth allows them to take amazing pictures of our weather systems. They can track hurricanes as they form over the oceans. Satellite-imaging has helped people to leave their homes and get out of a hurricane's path just in time.

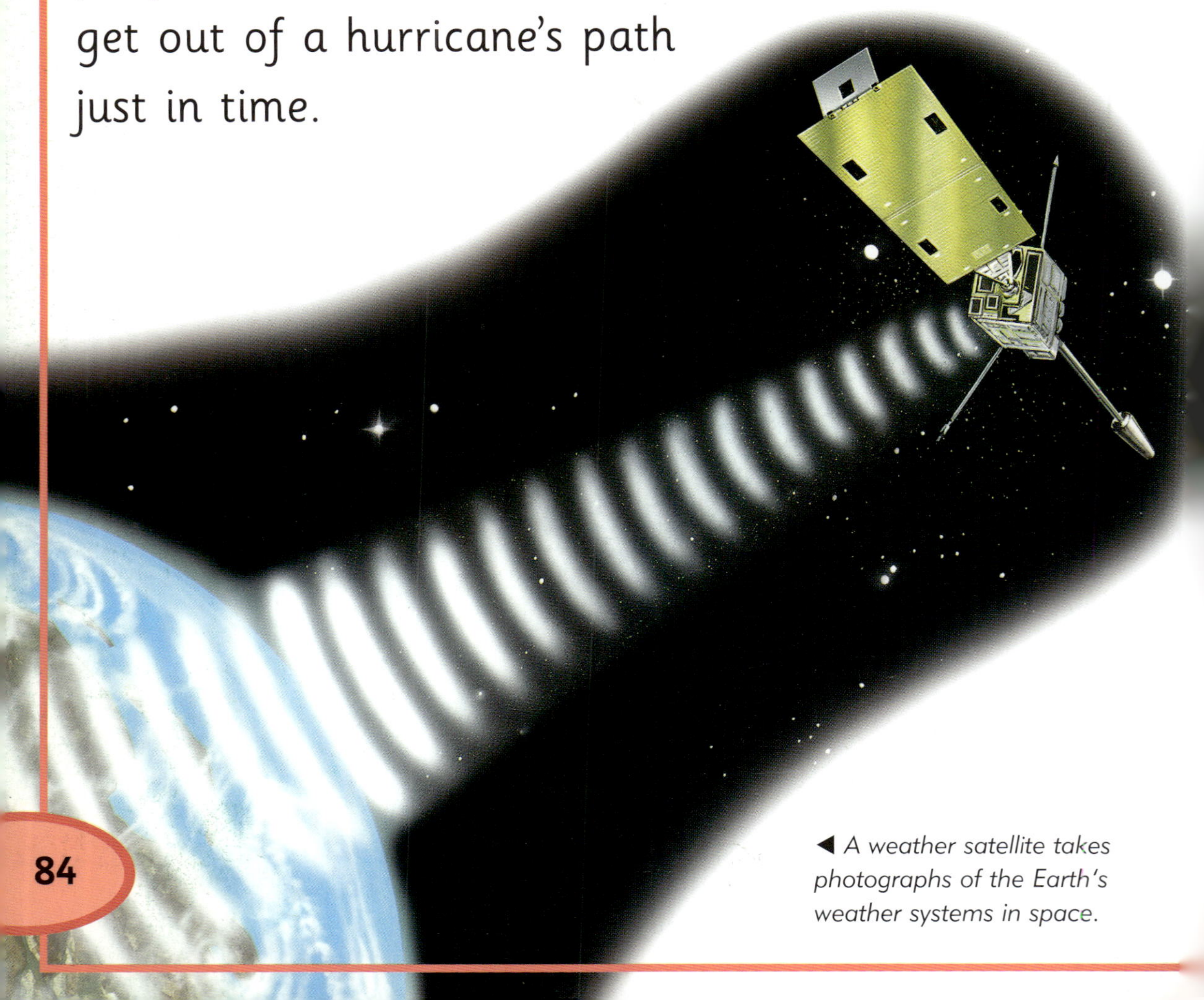

◀ *A weather satellite takes photographs of the Earth's weather systems in space.*

◀ *Weather balloons are hot-air balloons that are sent high into the atmosphere. Onboard equipment takes readings about the weather.*

▲ *Weather planes test the air ahead of the plane. This is* Snoopy*, one of the British weather planes.*

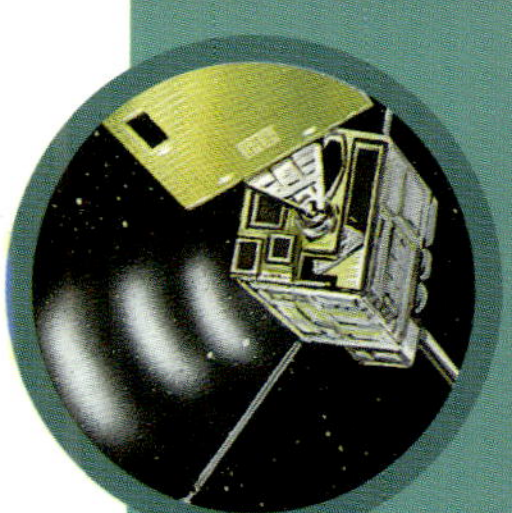

Satellites *take some of the best weather photographs.*

Weather balloons *are used around the world every day.*

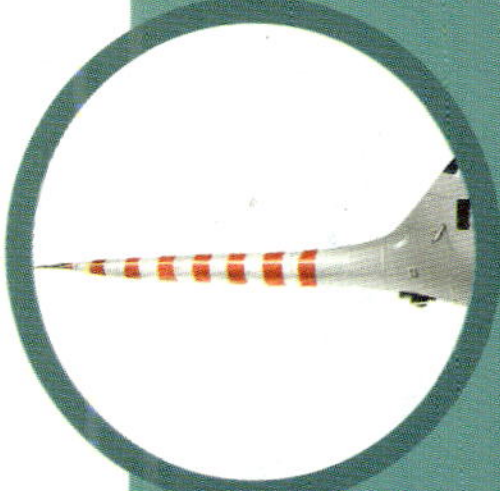

Snoopy's *long nose monitors the weather.*

Science and the future

Many modern machines and processes can cause damage to our environment and our health. The damage includes acid rain and pollution of rivers and lakes. Science can help to find solutions. New filters and chemicals called catalysts can cut down dangerous fumes from vehicles and power stations.

▶ *Recycling is an important area of science. Many materials, such as glass, can be recycled. This saves huge amounts of energy and raw materials.*

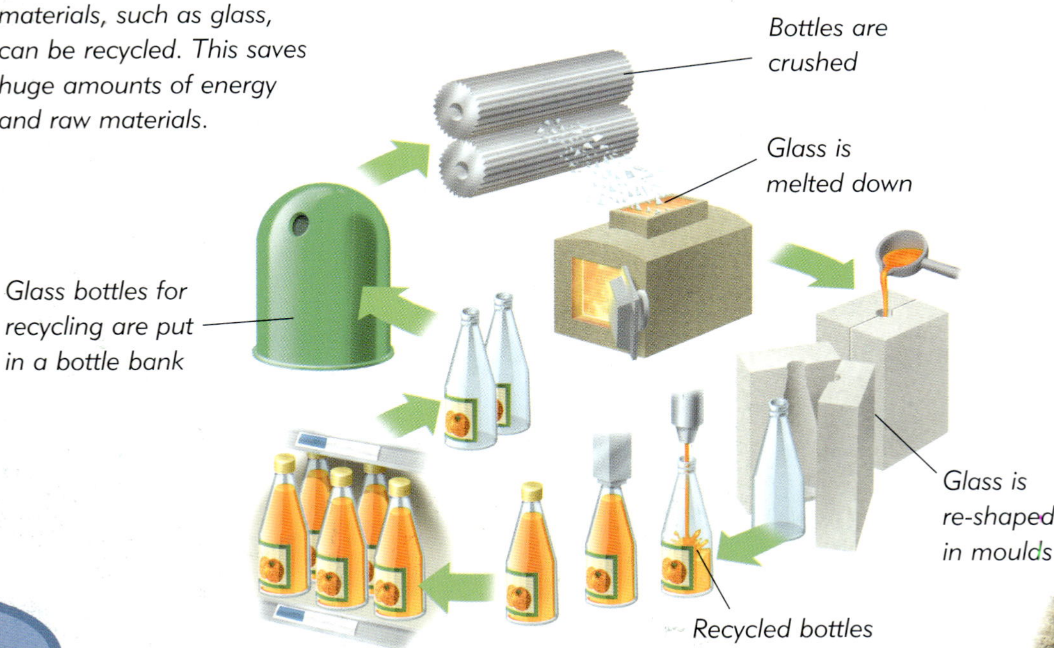

Which science?

If you become a scientist, which science would you like to study? See if you can guess what these sciences are:

1. *Meteorology* ***2.*** *Biology* ***3.*** *Astronomy* ***4.*** *Ecology*

1. *weather and climate* ***2.*** *animals, plants and other living things* ***3.*** *stars, planets and objects in space* ***4.*** *the way nature works*

▼ Fumes, waste and chemicals cause terrible pollution in many cities.

Vehicles *give out harmful exhaust fumes.*

Factories *fill the air with chemicals.*

Waste *is thrown into rivers and lakes, harming the wildlife.*

The dinosaur world

Dinosaurs were types of animals with scaly skin, called reptiles. They lived millions of years ago. There were many different kinds of dinosaurs, but they all died out long, long ago.

Corythosaurus *had a duck-like beak to scoop up plants.*

Tyrannosaurus *was a fierce meat-eater with powerful jaws.*

Triceratops *means 'three-horned face'.*

When were they around?

PALAEOZOIC ERA	MESOZOIC ERA	
PERMIAN PERIOD	TRIASSIC PERIOD	JURASSIC PERIOD

Erythrosuchus

Thrinaxodon

286 million years ago

The reptiles are becoming more important than the amphibians.

248 million years ago

The first proper dinosaurs appear. These were small, two-legged carnivores (meat-eaters) and larger herbivores (plant-eaters).

Riojasaurus

Plateosaurus

Barosaurus

Apatosaurus

Heterodontosaurus

208 million years ago

Many different dinosaurs lived at this time, includin[g] the giant plant-eaters like Barosaurus.

Dinosaurs lived between about 230 million and 65 million years ago. This vast length of time is called the Mesozoic Era. Dinosaurs were around for about 80 times longer than people have been on Earth!

MESOZOIC ERA

CRETACEOUS PERIOD

144 million years ago

During the last part of the Age of Dinosaurs, both giant carnivores and armoured herbivores were alive.

Tarbosaurus

Tyrannosaurus rex

Deinonychus

Spinosaurus

CENOZOIC ERA

TERTIARY PERIOD

Thylacosmilus, *meat-eating mammal*

Brontotherium, *plant-eating mammal*

Nesodon, *plant-eating mammal*

65 million years ago

The dinosaurs have all died out. The mammals, that have been around since the Triassic Period, become the main land animals.

Stegosaurus *was around for more than 20 million years. It was one of the longest lasting dinosaurs.*

Compsognathus *was one of the smallest dinosaurs known.*

Desmond's fun facts!

The name 'dinosaur' means 'terrible lizard'. But dinosaurs weren't lizards, and not all dinosaurs were terrible either!

Life before dinosaurs

Dinosaurs were not the first animals on Earth. Many other kinds of creatures lived before them, including many other types of reptiles. Over millions of years, one of these groups of reptiles probably changed very slowly, or evolved, into the first dinosaurs.

▼ Dimetrodon *was a fierce reptile that looked like a dinosaur – but it wasn't. It lived 270 million years ago, before the time of the dinosaurs.*

▲ Ornithosuchus *was an early thecodont. This was a carnivore (meat-eater) that walked on two legs, a cousin of the first dinosaurs.*

Erythrosuchus *was a crocodile that was around before the first dinosaurs.*

Therapsids *were reptiles with furry skin like mammals.*

Plants *such as tree ferns existed at this time.*

Test your memory!

1. *What type of animal was the dinosaur?*

2. *What is the name of the era in which dinosaurs lived?*

3. *Which dinosaur lasted for more than 20 million years?*

4. *Was* Compsognathus *one of the smallest or biggest dinosaurs known?*

1. *a reptile* ***2***. *the* Mesozoic *Era* ***3***. Stegosaurus ***4***. *the smallest*

Time for the dinosaurs

The earliest dinosaurs walked the Earth almost 230 million years ago. They lived in what is now Argentina, in South America. They included *Eoraptor* and *Herrerasaurus.* Both were slim and fast, and ran on their two back legs.

Make a dinosaur move!

You will need:

- *some stiff card*
- *safe scissors*
- *sticky tape* • *split pins*

1. *Cut out a model of Herrerasaurus. The head, body, arms and tail are one piece of card.*

2. *Cut out each leg from another piece. Fix the legs on either side of the hip area of the body using a split pin.*

3. *Move the angle of the head, body and tail to stand over the legs. This is how many dinosaurs moved, well balanced over their back legs.*

Herrerasaurus *had legs under its body, unlike other reptiles.*

The head *was long, with a bendy neck to look round for prey.*

The tail *helped it to keep its balance.*

Changing dinosaurs

As the early dinosaurs spread over the land, they began to change. This natural change in living things has happened since life began on Earth. New kinds of plants and animals appear, do well for a time, and then die out as yet more new kinds appear. This slow change of living things over time is called evolution.

▶ *Some kinds of dinosaur became larger and began to eat plants rather than animals.*

▼ Rutiodon *was a crocodile-like meat-eater*

Riojasaurus *weighed about one tonne – as much as a large family car of today.*

Plateosaurus *was one of the first big plant-eating dinosaurs.*

Desmond's fun facts!

Early plant-eating dinosaurs did not eat fruits or grasses – these hadn't appeared yet! Instead they ate plants such as horsetails and ferns.

Gentle giants

Mamenchisaurus grew up to 26 metres long. It lived in East Asia 160 million years ago

The true giants of the Age of Dinosaurs were the sauropods. These vast dinosaurs all had a small head, long neck, barrel-shaped body, long tail and four legs. The biggest sauropods included *Brachiosaurus*, *Barosaurus*, *Diplodocus* and *Argentinosaurus*.

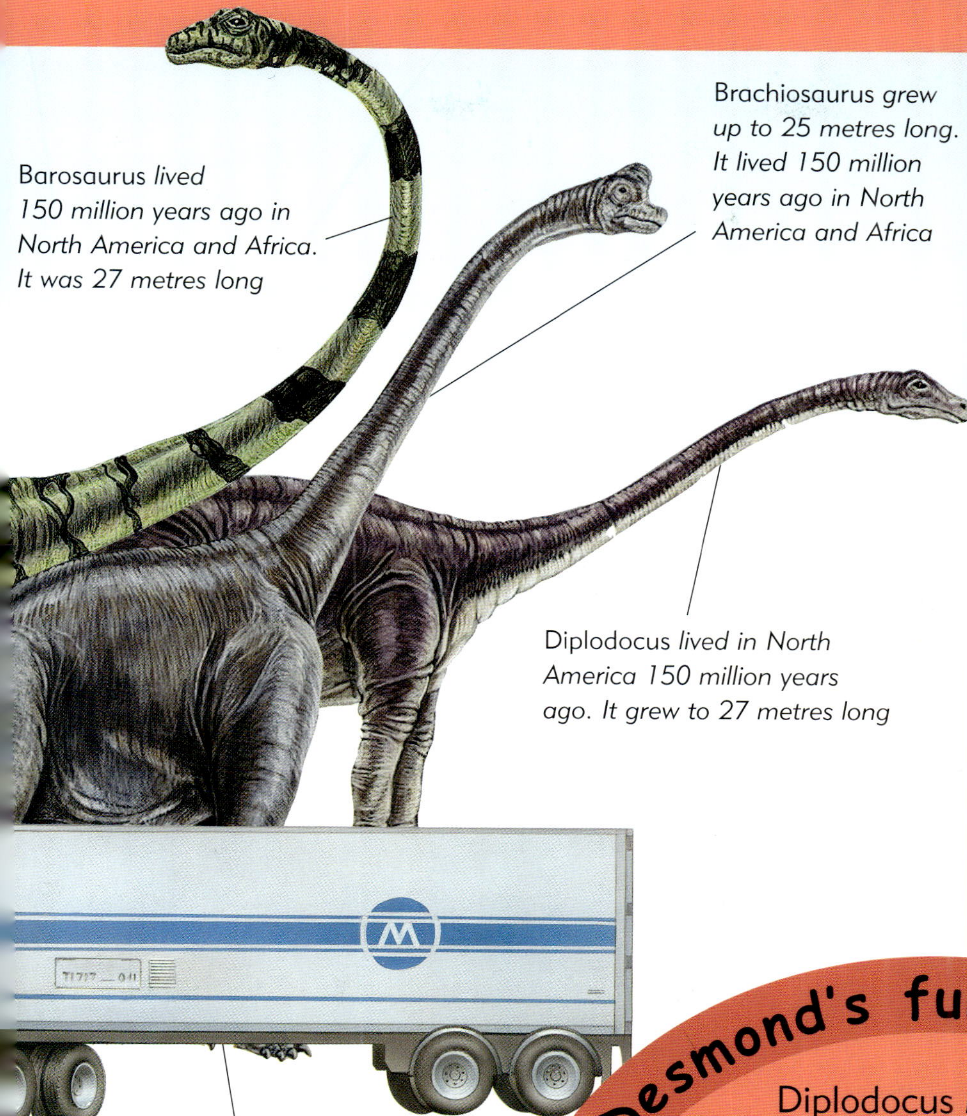

Barosaurus *lived 150 million years ago in North America and Africa. It was 27 metres long*

Brachiosaurus *grew up to 25 metres long. It lived 150 million years ago in North America and Africa*

Diplodocus *lived in North America 150 million years ago. It grew to 27 metres long*

This modern truck is to the same scale as these huge dinosaurs

Argentinosaurus *was the biggest sauropod – 40 metres long.*

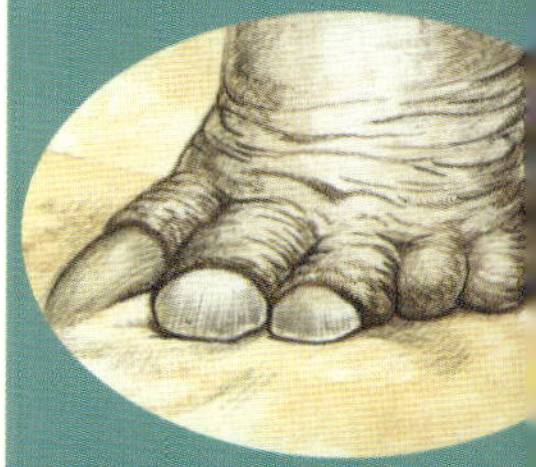

Sauropods *had flat claws which looked like toenails!*

Desmond's fun facts!

Diplodocus is also known as 'Old Whip-tail'! It could swish its long tail so hard and fast that it made an enormous CRACK like a whip.

Huge hunters

The biggest meat-eating dinosaurs were the largest predators (hunters) ever to have lived.

Different types came and went during the Age of Dinosaurs. One of the last dinosaurs was also one of the largest – *Tyrannosaurus.*

◀ Tyrannosaurus *had sharp teeth and powerful jaws.*

Gigantosaurus *was the biggest carnivore (meat-eater).*

Allosaurus *had long, strong back legs for fast running.*

Desmond's fun facts!

Some meat-eating dinosaurs not only bit their prey, but also each other! Fossils of several Tyrannosaurus had bite marks on the head.

Dinosaurs in battle

Some dinosaurs had body defences against predators. These might be large horns and spikes, or hard lumps of bone like armour-plating. Most armoured dinosaurs were plant-eaters. They had to defend themselves against big meat-eating dinosaurs such as *Tyrannosaurus.*

Design a dinosaur

Make an imaginary dinosaur! It might have the body armour and tail club of Euoplocephalus, or the horns and neck frill of Triceratops.

You can draw your dinosaur, make it out of pieces of card or from modelling clay. You can give it a made-up name, like 'Euoplo-ceratops' or 'Tri-cephalus'.

How well protected is your dinosaur? Is it anything like creatures of today?

Euoplocephalus *used the hard lump on its tail as a club for hitting enemies.*

Triceratops *had three horns for charging at predators.*

Protoceratops *may have used its neck frill to frighten off its enemies.*

Where did they all go?

All dinosaurs on Earth died out by 65 million years ago. There are dinosaur fossils in the rocks up to this time, but there are none after. There are, though, fossils of other creatures like fish and mammals. What happened to wipe out some of the biggest animals that ever lived? There are many ideas. It could have been one, or many, disasters.

▼ *The dinosaurs may have been killed by a giant lump of rock, called a meteorite.*

Meteorite smash!

You will need:

• plastic bowl • cooking flour • large pebble
• desk light • place where mess does not matter!

1. Ask an adult to help. Put the flour in the bowl. This is Earth's surface.

2. Place the desk light so it shines over the bowl. This is the Sun. The pebble is the meteorite from space.

3. WHAM! Drop the pebble into the bowl. See how the tiny bits of flour float in the air like a mist, making the 'Sun' dimmer. A real meteorite smash may have been the beginning of the end for the dinosaurs.

Volcanoes could have erupted and choked the dinosaurs to death.

Plagues of animals could have eaten all the dinosaurs' eggs.

A giant tidal wave could have drowned the dinosaurs.

What they left behind

We know about dinosaurs mainly from their fossils. Fossils took millions of years to form. Most fossils form on the bottoms of rivers or seas, where sand and mud can quickly cover them over and begin to preserve (keep) them.

▼ Fossils take millions of years to form. Firstly, an animal, like this trilobite, dies. Trilobites lived in the sea about 600 million years ago, long before the first dinosaurs.

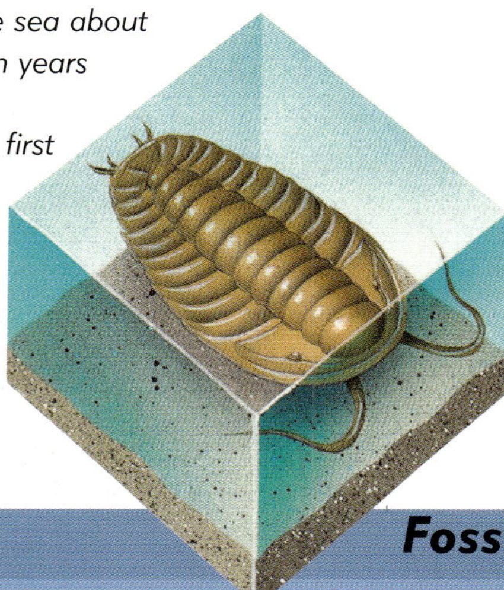

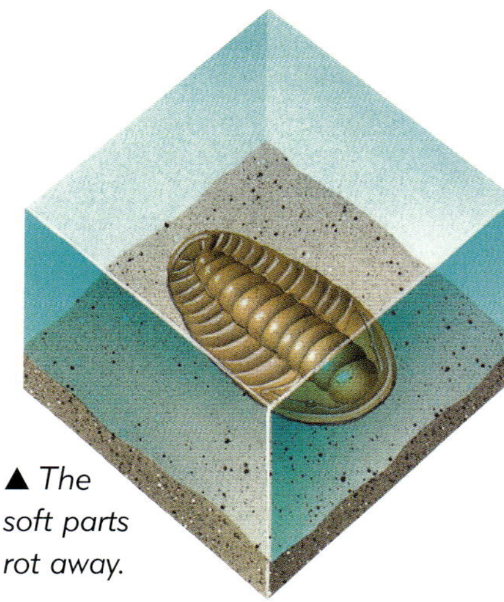

▲ The soft parts rot away.

Fossil quiz

What formed fossils?
Which body parts of a dinosaur were most likely to become fossils?
Remember, fossils form from the hardest bits that last long enough to become buried in the rocks and turned to stone.

skull bone muscle leg bone scaly skin blood claws eye teeth

skull bone, leg bone, teeth and claws are most likely to form fossils

▼ *The remaining shell is buried in mud.*

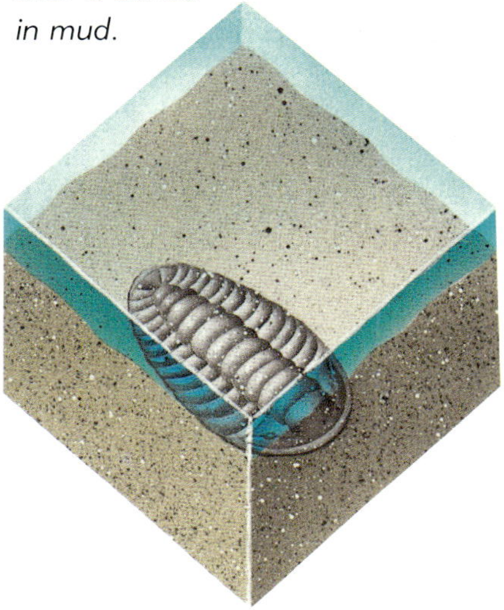

▲ *The mud turns to rock, which turns the shell to rock, and makes a fossil.*

▲ *The skull of Stegoceras was dome-shaped and thick. From this, scientists have guessed that they may have had head-butting contests.*

A Tyrannosaurus skull *shows its deadly, sharp teeth.*

Dinosaur footprints *became buried in the ground and turned into fossils.*

A dinosaur skin fossil *shows us how it was scaly, like reptile skin.*

Cold-blooded creatures

Reptiles and amphibians are cold-blooded animals. This means that they cannot control their body temperature like we can. A reptile's skin is dry and scaly and it spends most of its time on land. Most amphibians live in or around water and their skin is smooth and wet.

Crocodiles are the largest reptiles in the world.

The largest amphibian *in the world is a type of salamander.*

Tortoises are reptiles that live on land and eat plants.

Sea creatures

►▲ *When marine iguanas are not diving for food, they bask on the rocks that dot the island coastlines. The lizards' dark skin helps to absorb (take in) the Sun's heat.*

Cold-blooded creatures, such as reptiles, cannot control their body temperature like we can. This is why they prefer life on land, where it is easier for them to warm up. But there are some reptiles that have adapted to ocean life.

Oarfish grow up to 8 metres long! Their length protects them from hunters.

Sunfish are so-called because they sunbathe on the ocean surface.

A flounder's shape and colour help to camouflage (hide) it on the seabed.

▲ In a large group called a school, fish like these yellow snappers have less chance of being caught by hunters.

Awesome jaws!

Sharks don't have bones. Their skeletons are made of a gristly substance called cartilage. All sharks are meat-eaters. Some filter tiny prey from the water, or lie in wait for victims on the seabed. Others speed through the ocean after prey.

▲ *Great white sharks can speed through the water at 30 kilometres an hour.*

Test your memory!

1. *What length might an oarfish reach?*

2. *What is a large group of fish called?*

3. *How many types of fish are there in the sea?*

1. up to 8 metres **2.** a school

3. over 21,000 different types

▼ The blue shark can be dangerous and is known to attack humans.

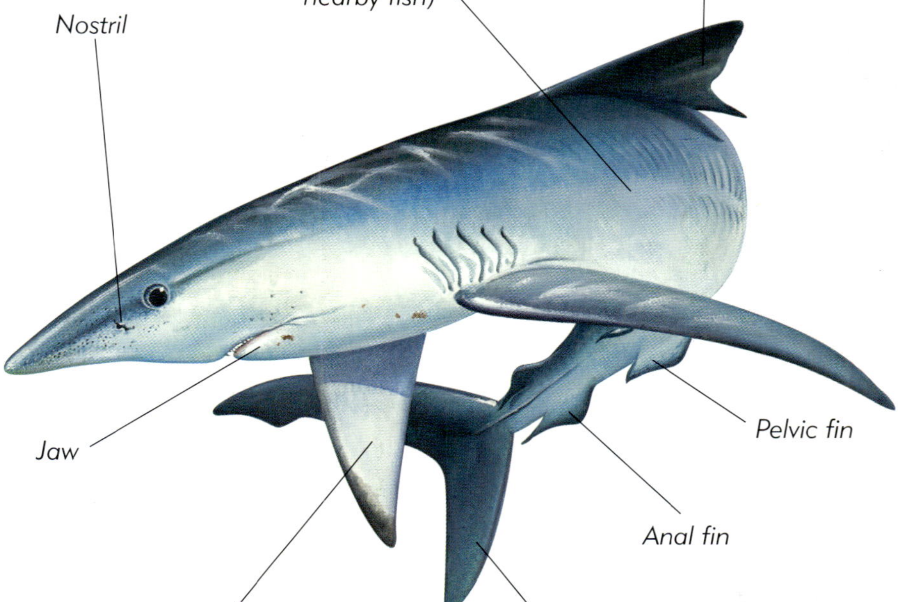

Basking sharks *eat huge amounts of tiny sea creatures called plankton.*

Hammerhead sharks *have a nostril and an eye on each end of their hammer-shaped head.*

Tiger sharks *may produce as many as 40 babies.*

Deep sea creatures

Few creatures can survive in the dark, icy-cold ocean depths. Food is so hard to find that creatures living there have very unusual features to help them survive. In the icy depths you will find glow-in-the-dark fish, fish with invisible teeth and even fish with their own fishing rods!

◀ *Black swallowers are just 25 centimetres long but can eat fish far bigger than themselves. Their loose jaws unhinge to fit over their prey and their body stretches to take in their huge meal.*

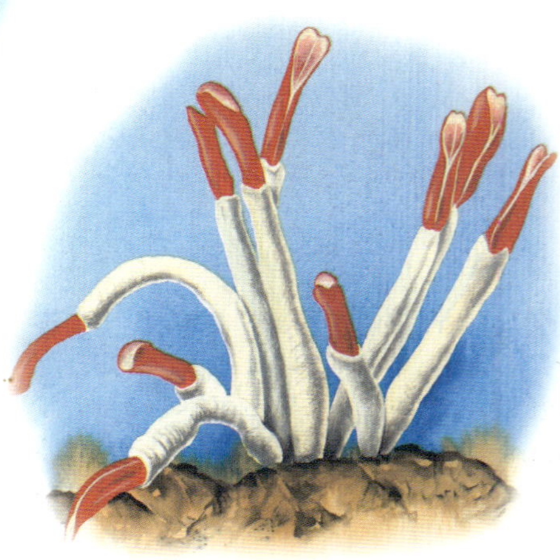

▶ *Giant tubeworms grow around hot spots on the ocean floor. They feed on tiny particles that they collect from the water.*

Test your memory!

1. *What are the largest reptiles in the world?*

2. *What do banded sea snakes use to stun prey?*

3. *Which is the biggest turtle in the world?*

4. *Where do marine iguanas live?*

Answers:

1. *crocodiles* **2.** *venom (poison)* **3.** *the leatherback turtle*

4. *on the Galapagos Islands in the Pacific Ocean*

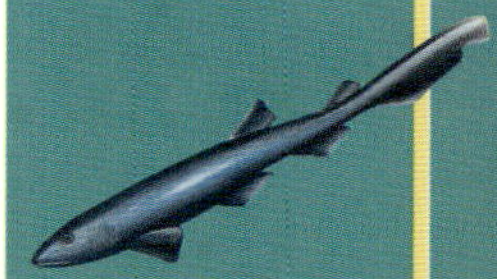

Cookiecutters *take biscuit-shaped bites out of their prey's body!*

Dragon fish *have light organs dotted along their sides and belly to tempt prey and confuse hunters.*

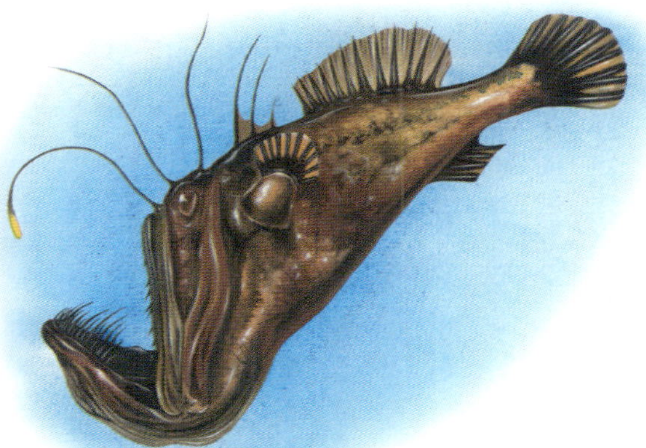

Lantern fish *have bodies that glow.*

◀ *The anglerfish has a stringy 'fishing rod' with a glowing tip that hangs above its jaw. This attracts small fish to its mouth, which it then catches and eats.*

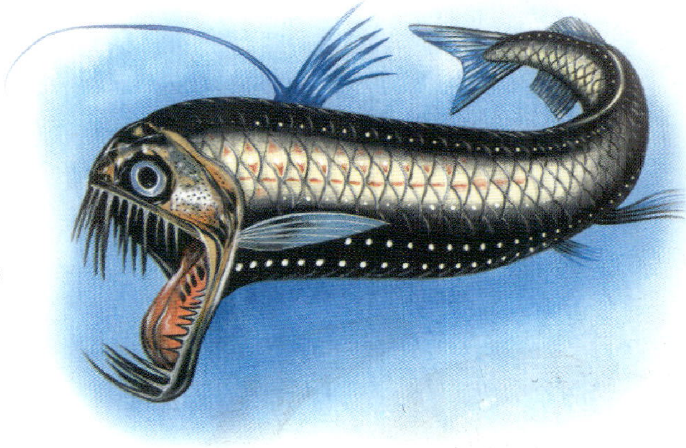

▶ *A viperfish's long, snake-like fangs are invisible in the dark. Its prey does not realize it has entered the viperfish's mouth until it is too late!*

What are mammals?

Mammals are warm-blooded animals with a bony skeleton and fur or hair. Being warm-blooded means that a mammal can keep its body at a constant temperature, even if the weather is very cold. There is one sort of mammal you know very well – you!

The Eurasian otter *has webbed feet to help it swim.*

Meerkats *live together in family groups.*

The Western tarsier *sleeps during the day and hunts at night.*

The world of mammals

There are nearly 4500 different types of mammal. Most have babies which grow inside the mother's body. While a baby mammal grows, a special organ called a placenta supplies it with food and oxygen from the mother's body. These mammals are called placental mammals.

▲ *Olive baboons live in Africa in groups called troops of between 20 and 150 animals.*

◀ *Marsupials give birth to young that finish growing in a pouch. The tiny baby kangaroo makes its own way to the safety of its mother's pouch, where it begins to feed on a teat.*

The echidna *is one of two groups of mammals that lay eggs instead of giving birth.*

Bats *are the only mammals that are able to fly.*

▲ *The fallow deer, like all deer, has a good sense of smell. This is so that it can sniff the air for the scent of an enemy.*

Bernie's fun facts!

Bears love honey. They tear bees' nests apart to get at the honey – but don't seem to mind getting stung!

Tallest and smallest

The blue whale is the biggest mammal. It spends all its life in the sea. It can measure more than 33.5 metres long – that is as long as seven family cars parked end to end. The elephant is the biggest land mammal, while the smallest mammal in the world is the tiny hog-nosed bat.

◀ *Gorillas are the biggest primates. Primates are the group of mammals to which chimpanzees and humans belong.*

▶ *The tiny hog-nosed bat is only three centimetres long. It weighs only two grams – less than a teaspoon of rice!*

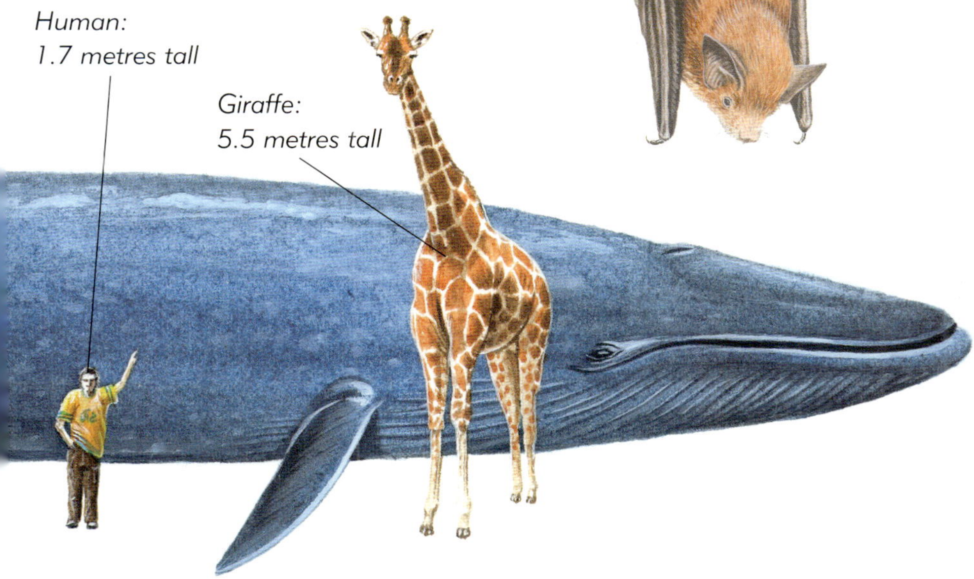

The mouse deer *is the smallest deer – it is only the size of a hare.*

The capybara *is the largest rodent. Rodents are the group that includes rats and mice.*

The pygmy shrew *is the smallest land mammal.*

Test your memory!

1. *How many types of mammal are there?*
2. *Where does a baby kangaroo finish growing?*
3. *Which is the only mammal that can fly?*
4. *What is the special organ that supplies food and oxygen to a baby mammal in the mother's body?*

1. nearly 4500 **2.** in its mother's pouch **3.** the bat **4.** the placenta

Top racers

▼ *The cheetah's long legs and muscular body help it to run fast. The long tail balances the body while it is running.*

The cheetah can run faster than any other animal. It can move at about 100 kilometres an hour, but it cannot run this fast for long. The cheetah uses its speed to catch other animals to eat. Other mammals, such as the brown hare or the pronghorn, run fast to escape their enemies.

The pronghorn *is one of the fastest mammals in North America.*

The brown hare *has strong back legs to help it move quickly.*

The red kangaroo *is a champion jumper.*

Speed demons!

How do you compare to the fastest mammal on Earth?

1. *Ask an adult to help. Measure how far you can run in ten seconds. Times this by six.*

2. *Times the answer by 60. This will tell you how many metres you can run in an hour.*

3. *Divide this by 1000. You will get your speed in kilometres an hour. You will find it will be far less than the cheetah's 100 kilometres an hour!*

Snow mammals

The polar bear is the biggest land mammal in the Arctic. The Arctic is a cold place at the very top of the world. The polar bear's thick fur helps to keep it warm.

The coats of some Arctic animals change colour. In winter, the Arctic hare has white fur to help hide it among the snow.

In summer its coat turns brown.

Bernie's fun facts!

The polar bear needs its thick fur to keep out the Arctic cold – even the soles of its feet are furry!

▼ *Lemmings are rodents which live mostly in the cold north. They build nests under the snow in winter. During the summer, they nest underground.*

▼ The leopard seal lives in the Antarctic, at the very bottom of the world. It is a fierce hunter and eats penguins, fish and even other seals. There are no land mammals in the Antarctic.

The male walrus *has long teeth called tusks, for digging shellfish from the seabed.*

The musk ox *has a long shaggy coat to help it survive the Arctic cold.*

The snowshoe hare *has a brown coat in summer, which turns white in winter.*

Plant-eaters

Plant-eaters must spend much of their time eating in order to get enough nourishment (goodness from food). A zebra, for example, spends at least half its day munching grass. The good side to being a plant-eater, though, is that the animal does not have to chase and fight for its food as hunters do.

▼ *Plants are the main foods for most monkeys. Some will also eat insects and other small creatures.*

Rabbits *have strong teeth for eating leaves and bark.*

The Queensland blossom bat *feeds on flower pollen and nectar.*

◀ *Plant-eaters, such as zebras, provide food for meat-eaters, such as lions. This is part of nature's 'food chain'.*

Bernie's fun facts!

Some monkeys have a long tail which they use for climbing – like an extra arm or leg!

Hungry hunters

Mammals which hunt and kill other creatures are called carnivores. Examples of carnivores are animals such as lions, tigers, wolves and dogs. Many carnivores do not have to hunt every day – one kill will last them for several days.

▶ *The tiger is the biggest of the big cats and an expert hunter. Buffalo, deer and wild pigs are its usual prey (victims).*

Make a food chain

Make your own food chain.

1. Draw a picture of a carnivore, such as a lion, and tie it to a piece of string.
2. Draw a picture of an animal that the lion catches, such as a zebra. Hang that from the lion picture.
3. Lastly, draw some grass and plants (the food of the zebra). Hang that from the picture of the zebra.

▲ *Bears are carnivores, but most bears, except for the polar bear, eat more plants than meat. Brown bears eat fish, fruit, nuts and insects.*

Hunting dogs *hunt in packs (groups), so that together they can kill a larger animal.*

The wild boar *is related to the farmyard pig. It eats plants and sometimes small animals.*

The female lion (lioness) *does most of the hunting for the family.*

Fins and flippers

Most swimming mammals have flippers and fins instead of legs. Seals and sea lions have paddle-like flippers. They use them to drag themselves along on land, as well as for swimming in water. Whales never come to land. They swim by moving their tails up and down and using their front flippers to steer.

▶ *The Weddell seal can dive deeper than any other seal.*

▶ *The harp seal lives in the Arctic Ocean.*

▶ *The northern fur seal has larger rear flippers than other fur seals.*

The bowhead whale *uses filters in its mouth to catch food.*

The narwhal *has a long tooth growing out from its lip.*

The killer whale *is the largest member of the dolphin family.*

Test your memory!

1. *What is the name of animals that eat meat?*
2. *Which is the biggest of all big cats?*
3. *What does the Queensland blossom bat eat?*
4. *Which mammal is the wild boar related to?*

***1.** carnivores **2.** the tiger **3.** flower pollen and nectar **4.** the pig*

Baby mammals

Female mammals feed their young on the milk they produce. Some young mammals, such as antelopes, have to be up and running less than an hour after birth or they will be killed by predators (hunters).

Other mammals, such as rabbits, are born blind and helpless.

Test your memory!

1. Which mammal is the largest member of the dolphin family?

2. Which is the biggest land mammal?

3. Which mammal can run the fastest?

4. What kind of mammal is a capybara?

1. the killer whale **2.** the elephant **3.** the cheetah **4.** a rodent

The Virginia opossum has more babies than any other mammal – as many as 21.

The elephant has the longest pregnancy of any mammal – about twenty months.

A baby panda stays with its mother for up to two years.

◀ The female puma, or mountain lion, gives birth to cubs (babies) with spotted fur. The spots disappear as the cubs grow older.

Birds everywhere

A bird has two legs, a pair of wings and a body that is covered with feathers. Birds are, perhaps, the animals we see most often in the wild. They live all over the world – everywhere from Antarctica to the hottest deserts and rainforests.

The greater flamingo uses its beak to filter food from shallow water.

The ostrich has strong legs for fast running.

A hornbill has a horn-like growth on its beak called a casque.

The bird world

There are more than 9000 different types, or species, of bird. These have been organized by scientists into groups called orders, which contain many different species. The largest order is called the passerines, also known as perching or song birds. These include common birds such as robins.

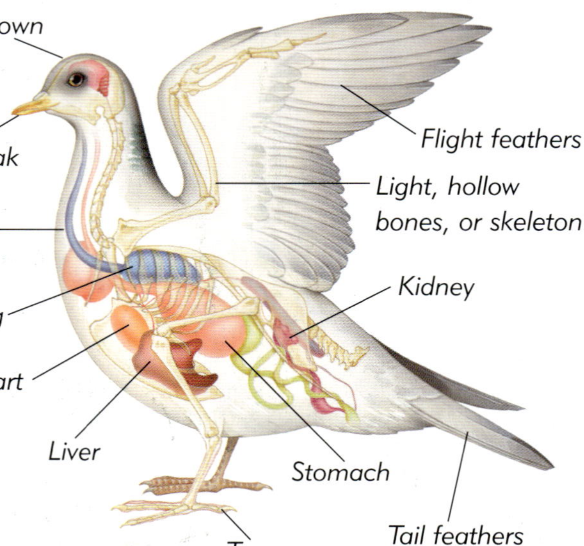

▼ *Pigeons have strong wing muscles to help them escape from hunters.*

▲ *All birds lay eggs. The egg protects the growing young. The parent birds, such as this song thrush, keep the egg safe and warm.*

The goshawk *is a hunting bird, or bird of prey. It can kill an animal as big as a rabbit.*

The whistling swan *is thought to have the most feathers – more than 25,000.*

Peggy's fun facts!

Bird brains aren't stupid – ravens and pigeons can work out simple sums, while parrots can copy human speech!

Biggest and smallest

The world's largest bird is the ostrich. It stands up to 2.75 metres tall and weighs up to 115 kilograms – twice as much as an average adult human. The smallest bird is the tiny bee hummingbird, which is only about five centimetres long – scarcely bigger than a real bee.

▼ *Ostriches live in the grasslands of Africa, where they feed on leaves, flowers and seeds.*

▲ *The wandering albatross has the longest wings of any bird. When outstretched, they measure as much as 3.3 metres from tip to tip.*

The bee hummingbird *feeds on flower nectar, as do other hummingbirds.*

The Andean condor *is the biggest type of vulture.*

The collared falconet *is the smallest bird of prey.*

Test your memory!

1. *How many types of bird are there?*
2. *What is the horn-like growth on a hornbill's beak called?*
3. *What is the largest order of birds called?*
4. *What is another name for a hunting bird?*

1. *more than 9000* ***2.*** *a casque* ***3.*** *the passerines* ***4.*** *a bird of prey*

Fast fliers

The fastest flying bird is the peregrine falcon. It hunts other birds in the air and makes amazing high-speed dives to catch its prey. Ducks and geese are also fast fliers. Many of them, such as the eider duck, can fly at speeds of over 65 kilometres an hour.

Feed the birds!

In winter, there is not much food for birds. You can make your own food cake to help them.

You will need:

- 225g of suet, lard or dripping
- 500g of seeds, nuts, biscuit crumbs and other scraps.

1. Ask an adult for help. Melt the fat, and mix it with the seed and scraps.
2. Pour the mixture into an old yogurt pot (or similar container) and leave it to cool and harden.
3. Remove the cake from the pot. Make a hole through the cake and put a string through the hole. Hang it from a tree outside.

Hummingbirds beat their wings more than 50 times a second as they hover in the air.

Mergansers are ducks which can dive very quickly into the water to catch fish.

▲ The swift spends most of its life in the air.

Swallows twist and zigzag in the air as they fly.

▶ The greater roadrunner is a fast mover on land. It can fly but seems to prefer running!

Bird homes

Birds make nests in which to lay their eggs and keep them safe. Nests can be made of twigs, leaves, mud or even saliva or spit. They are built in a variety of places, such as in trees, beside the water or in the walls of buildings.

▶ *The bald eagle makes one of the biggest nests of any bird. It is made of sticks and built in a tree or on rocks.*

Peggy's fun facts!

Sometimes people collect the nests of cave swiftlets to make bird's nest soup!

▲ *The mallee fowl makes a nest mound made of plants covered with sand. If the mound cools, the male bird adds more sand. If it gets too hot, he makes some holes to let warmth out.*

A weaver bird *twists strips of leaves around a branch to make its nest.*

A cuckoo *lays her eggs in the nests of other birds.*

The cave swiftlet *makes a nest from its own saliva or spit.*

Flying away

When the weather gets cold, many birds migrate. This means they leave to fly to warmer countries. Here, the birds will find food to eat while they lay their eggs and raise their young.

▼ The Canada goose spends the summer in the Arctic and the winter in North America.

▶ The Arctic tern travels further than any other bird. Every autumn, it flies from the top of the world, the Arctic, to the bottom, the Antarctic.

▲ When birds migrate, they often fly together in a V-shape.

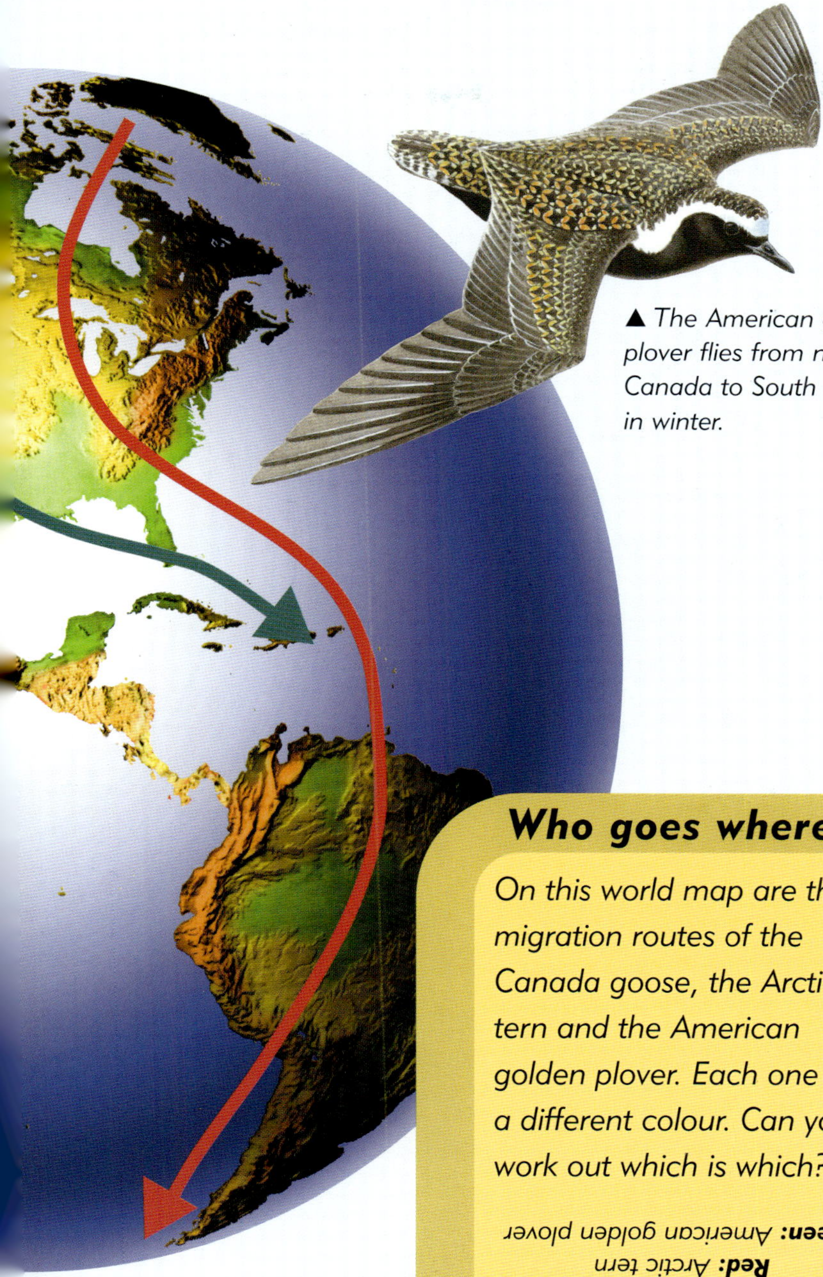

▲ *The American golden plover flies from northern Canada to South America in winter.*

Canada geese *make loud, honking calls as they fly.*

The American golden plover *nests in the tundra, a cold Arctic region.*

The Arctic tern *sees more daylight than any other creature.*

Who goes where?

On this world map are the migration routes of the Canada goose, the Arctic tern and the American golden plover. Each one is a different colour. Can you work out which is which?

Blue: *Canada goose*
Red: *Arctic tern*
Green: *American golden plover*

Fierce hunters

Eagles, hawks and owls are all birds of prey. These are birds who hunt other animals. The golden eagle is one of the fiercest of all birds of prey. When it spies a victim, it dives down and seizes its prey in its powerful claws, called talons.

Word scramble

Unscramble these words to find the names of four different birds of prey:

***1**. GALEE*   ***3**. LOW*

***2**. KHAW*   ***4**. NEARV*

1. EAGLE **2.** HAWK **3.** OWL **4.** RAVEN

▼ *The golden eagle can soar for hours on its huge wings, searching for prey such as rabbits, birds and mice.*

Steller's sea eagle *swoops down to the ocean and seizes fish in its sharp claws.*

The raven *mainly hunts rats and mice, but it can kill larger animals, such as rabbits.*

The crested serpent eagle *feeds mostly on snakes and lizards.*

Family life

Each species of bird has its own way of caring for its young. Emperor penguins lay eggs and rear (bring up) their young on the Antarctic ice. Hawks and falcons look after their young and bring them food for many weeks. Other birds, such as ducks and geese, are able to run around and find food as soon as they hatch.

▼ *While the male penguin incubates the egg (keeps it warm), he does not eat. When the chick hatches, the female returns to take over its care.*

Swans *carry their young, called cygnets, on their back as they swim.*

Sparrowhawks *are born blind and helpless, so need their parents' care for many weeks.*

◀ *A female mallard leads her ducklings in the water.*

Peggy's fun facts!

Penguins huddle together for warmth while they incubate their eggs. They take it in turns to stand on the outside and take the force of the cold winds.

Birds and people

Many kinds of birds are now endangered species. This means that they are in danger of dying out. The parrot family was once common in the rainforests. Now many parrots are rare, as people have been stealing them from the wild to sell.

▶ *Starlings are very common city birds. They can eat many foods and nest almost anywhere.*

Parrots *are taken from the wild to be put in cages and sold as pets.*

Chickens *are reared for their meat and eggs.*

Peggy's fun facts!

Sometimes crows place walnuts in front of cars. The cars move over the nuts, breaking the shells for them to eat!

Creepy-crawlies

Insects form the largest of all animal groups, with millions of different kinds, or species. But not all creepy-crawlies are insects. Spiders belong to a different group called arachnids.

Millepedes *belong to yet another group to spiders and insects.*

Tarantulas *have eight legs, like all arachnids.*

Wood-ants *are typical insects, with six legs and three body sections.*

Insects everywhere!

Insects, such as the housefly, are among the most widespread of all animals. There are many other members of the fly group, such as bluebottles, horseflies, craneflies ('daddy-long-legs') and fruitflies. Other common insects include ladybirds, butterflies, ants and earwigs.

▼ *There are many different kinds of butterflies and moths. The white butterfly is not usually welcome in the garden. Their young, called caterpillars, eat the leaves of gardeners' plants.*

Insect-spotting

Have you seen any insects so far today?

On a warm summer's day you probably see many kinds of insects. On a cold winter's day there are fewer insects about. Most are hiding away or have not yet hatched out of their eggs.

The scorpionfly *has a harmless sting on a long, curved tail.*

Ants *are fine in the garden or wood, but are pests in the house.*

The earwig *likes dark, damp corners – not ears or wigs!*

Flapping around

Most kinds of insects have two pairs of wings. An insect's wings are attached to the middle part of its body, the thorax. A large butterfly flaps its wings once or twice each second. Some tiny flies flap their wings about 1000 times each second.

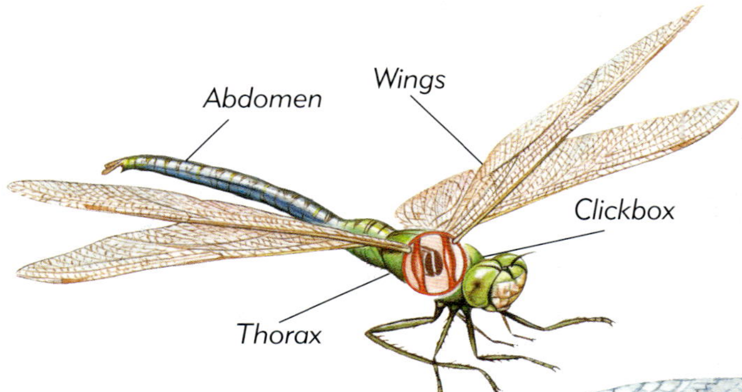

▶ *The clickbox is like a box with strong walls. Muscles pull to make the walls click in and out, which makes the wings flick up and down.*

Make a flapping fly!

You will need:

- some stiff card
- tissue paper
- round-ended scissors
- sticky tape

1. Ask an adult for help. Carefully cut out the card to make a box with two open ends, as shown.

2. Attach strips of stiff card to the sides to make struts for the wings. Make the rest of the wings from tissue paper.

3. Hold the box as shown. Move the top and bottom walls in, then out. This bends the side walls and makes the wings flap, just like a real insect.

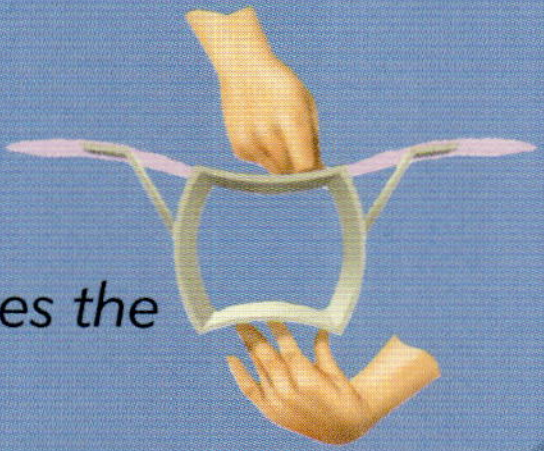

◀ *The dragonfly is a fast and fierce flying hunter.*

***The apollo butterfly** is a strong flier, flapping over hills and mountains.*

***The firefly** flashes bright lights as it flies to help attract a mate.*

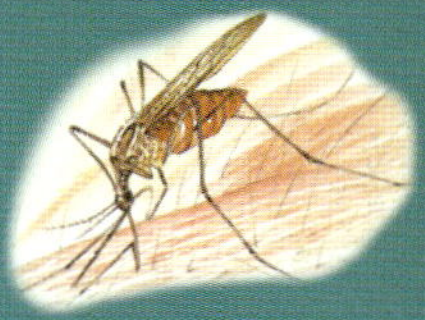

***Mosquitoes** are one of the smallest flying insects.*

Speedy bugs

Some insects hardly ever fly or leap. They prefer to run, and run, and run...all day, and even all night too. Among the champion insect runners are cockroaches. Most scurry speedily across the ground on long legs.

▲ *Cockroaches have low, flat bodies. They can race into narrow holes, under stones and into furniture – and beds!*

Stonefly nymphs *run around on riverbeds searching for food.*

The devil's coach-horse *is a type of beetle that walks long distances to find food.*

Bella's fun facts!

For its size, a green tiger beetle runs ten times as fast as a person! It runs about 60–70 centimetres a second. That is like a human sprinter running 100 metres in 1 second!

Bites and stings

Most insects may be small, but they are among the fiercest hunters in the animal world. Many have mouthparts shaped like spears or saws, which they use for grabbing and tearing up victims. Some have very powerful bites and poison stings.

▶ *The praying mantis is one of the most powerful insect hunters. It gets its name because it holds its front legs like a person with hands together in prayer.*

▼ *Wasp's head*

Antenna detects smells

Jaws used for digging and cutting up food

Test your memory!

1. What kind of insect is the devil's coach-horse?
2. Which insect is one of the speediest runners?
3. How many legs do arachnids have?
4. Which insect flashes a bright light as it flies?

1. a beetle **2.** cockroach
3. eight **4.** the firefly

The lacewing is a fearsome hunter of small creatures.

Bombardier beetles squirt out a horrible liquid that stings their enemies.

The hornet is a large wasp with a very painful sting.

▼ *The mantis stays perfectly still, then when a victim comes near – SNAP!*

Insect homes

Some insects live together in huge groups called colonies, which are like insect cities. There are four main types of insects which form colonies. One is the termites. The other three are bees, wasps and ants.

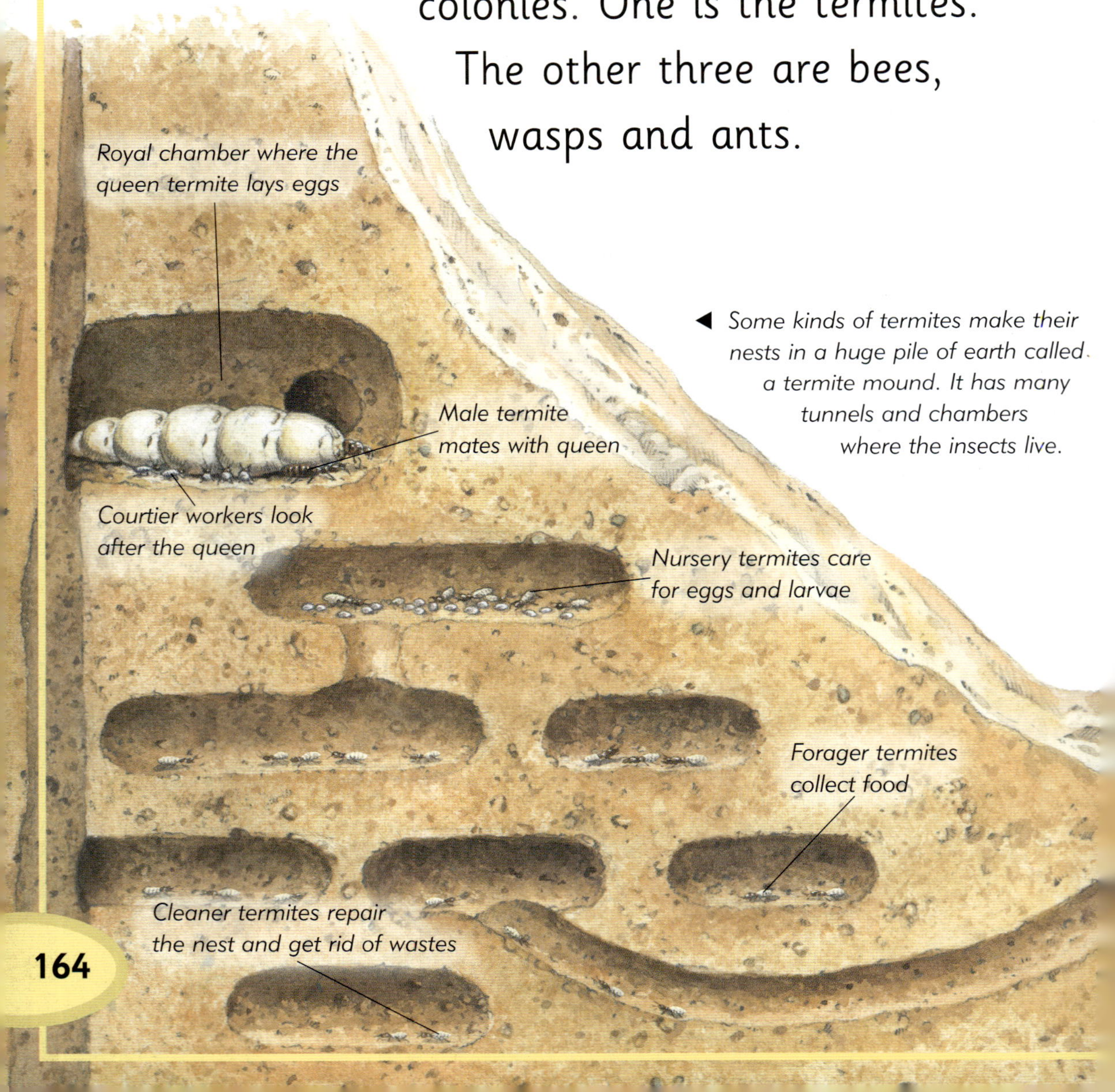

◀ *Some kinds of termites make their nests in a huge pile of earth called a termite mound. It has many tunnels and chambers where the insects live.*

► *Some wasps build nests of paper, made from chewed-up bits of plants and wood.*

Leaf-cutter ants *make nests with leaves to grow fungus, which they eat.*

Bees *live in nests with around 50,000 others.*

Ant-lion larva *lives in sand or soil, waiting for its prey to pass.*

Test your memory!

1. *Finish the name of this insect predator: the praying...?*

2. *What kind of insect is a hornet?*

3. *Does an insect's antenna let it breathe or smell?*

4. *Is the thorax the top, middle or bottom part of an insect's body?*

1. *mantis* **2.** *a wasp*
3. *smell* **4.** *the middle*

What is a spider?

A spider has eight legs. So it is not an insect. It is a type of animal called an arachnid. All spiders are deadly hunters. They have large jaws which they use to kill their prey. They inject a poison to kill the victim. Like spiders, scorpions, mites and ticks have eight legs. So they are also arachnids.

▶ *The Australian redback spider is one of the most deadly of a group called widow spiders.*

Make a spiders web

You will need:

- piece of card
- round-ended scissors
- reel of cotton
- PVA glue

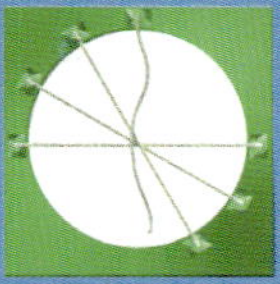

1. Ask an adult for help. Cut a large hole out of the card. Stretch a piece of cotton across the hole and stick both ends to the card.

2. Do the same again several times at different angles. Make sure all the threads cross at the centre of the hole.

3. Starting at the centre, glue a long piece of thread to each of the threads. Work your way round in a spiral until you reach the edge. That's the way that real spiders make webs!

Stage one
A spider starts a web by building a bridge.

Stage two
It adds more threads to make a strong framework.

Stage three
The spider fills the frame with circular threads.

▼ *The bolas spider catches insects flying past with its own kind of fishing line.*

The spider world

Not all spiders catch their prey using webs. Some spiders, such as the wolf spider, run fast and chase tiny prey such as beetles and slugs. Others, such as the trapdoor spider, hide away until an animal passes, then jump out to grab their victim.

▼ *Tarantulas are strong enough to catch big insects, such as this grasshopper, and even small birds.*

▼ *The gold leaf crab spider looks like a small crab. Here, it has caught a honeybee. Its poison paralyzes (freezes) the bee so it cannot escape.*

The trapdoor spider *waits behind a door made of silk for its prey to pass.*

Wolf spiders *have long, strong legs for fast running.*

Bella's fun facts!

Tarantulas are huge spiders from South America and Africa. Stretch your hand out and it still would not be as big as some of these giants!

A sting in the tail

A scorpion has eight legs. It is not an insect. Like a spider, it is an arachnid. Scorpions live in warm parts of the world, such as rainforests and deserts. The scorpion has crablike pincers to grab its prey, and powerful jaws to chop it up.

▼ *This scorpion has caught a katydid, a type of grasshopper, by paralyzing it with its sting.*

Spider scramble!

Unscramble the words below to find the names of four types of spider:

1. *FLOW* **2.** *BRAC*

3. *NATRALUTA* **4.** *WODIW*

1. *WOLF* **2.** *CRAB*
3. *TARANTULA* **4.** *WIDOW*

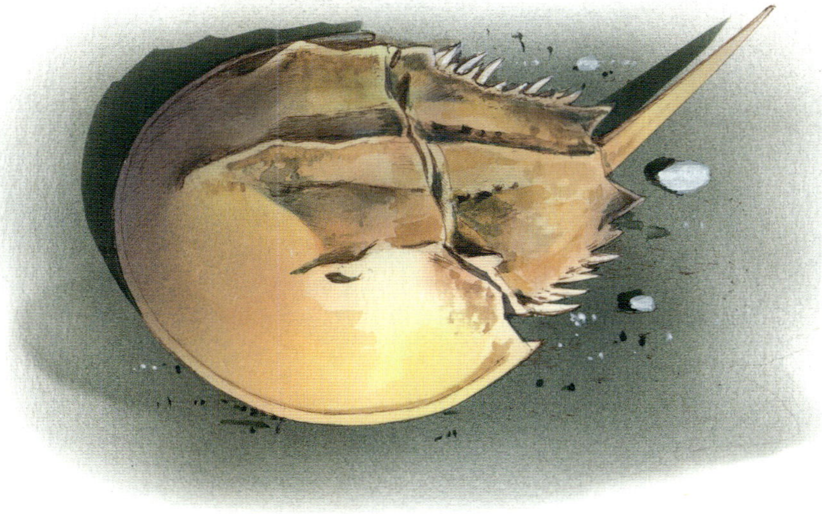

▲ *The king crab has eight legs, so is an arachnid. It has a domed shell and spiky tail, but is harmless.*

The sun-spider *is a fierce hunter with a poisonous bite.*

The false scorpion *does not have a sting in its tail and is very small.*

The black widow *is a dangerous spider – its bite can kill people.*

Hunter gatherers

The Stone Age began about two and a half million years ago and lasted tens of thousands of years. During this time, people worked out better ways of hunting and gathering food and eventually learned how to farm. They also made strange stone arrangements. These were possibly places where religious ceremonies were held.

▼ *Towards the end of the Stone Age in Britain, some people made a ring of massive stones at Stonehenge.*

▶ *Stone Age people were the first to use stone to make tools and weapons for hunting and gathering food.*

◀ *The stones at Stonehenge were arranged so the Sun shone into the entrance on the morning of the summer solstice (longest day of summer).*

Axe-heads *were made from flint (a type of stone).*

Antler picks *were used to pick flint from surrounding chalk.*

Some of the stones *at Stonehenge were carried from a quarry in Wales, 385 kilometres away.*

Early Americans

The first American people came from Asia. About 20,000 years ago, the sea level was lower, leaving a strip of land uncovered between the two continents of Asia and North America. People wandered across this strip of land, and gradually spread out through America.

▼ *Men of the Plains tribes hunted herds of buffalo on the prairies (grasslands).*

▶ *This map shows where the various Native American peoples lived.*

◀ *The Hopi peoples lived in the Southwest, a vast, dry area of America. They grew crops along the rivers.*

Native Americans *lived by hunting and fishing.*

Buffalo *provided meat for eating and skin for making clothes.*

The Hopi *dressed in skirts made of leather and woven grasses.*

Life on the Nile

Without the waters of the river Nile, Egyptian civilization might never have existed. The Nile provided water for drinking, watering crops and for transport. Over 7000 years ago, people from central Africa began to arrive in Egypt and settle along the banks of the Nile.

Boats *were the best way to get around.*

Papyrus reeds *had many uses, from making boats to shoes.*

Temples *were built to worship the Egyptian gods.*

Powerful pharaohs

The rulers of ancient Egypt were called pharaohs. The word 'pharaoh' means great house. The pharaoh was the most important and powerful person in the country. He owned all the land and ordinary people believed that he was a god.

▶ *These people are paying tribute to the pharaoh. This means that they have come to give him presents and tell him how great he is!*

◀ *Here the pharaoh is holding the symbols of his rule, the hook and flail.*

Ramses II *ruled for over 60 years. He was a great builder and a brave soldier.*

Tutankhamun *was only nine years old when he became pharaoh.*

Cleo's fun facts!

Women courtiers sometimes wore hair cones made of scented animal fat. When it melted it made their hair sweet-smelling – and greasy!

Ruling families

Over 30 different dynasties ruled ancient Egypt. A dynasty is a line of rulers from the same family. The pharaoh often married a sister or half-sister, so that the blood of the royal family remained pure.

Cleo's fun facts!

Queen Hatsheput wore the royal crown and the ceremonial beard when she became pharaoh!

▼ *Cleopatra was one of the last rulers of Egypt. She fell in love with Roman general, Julius Caesar, and later married Mark Antony (shown here).*

Queen Hatshepsut *ruled Egypt for 20 years.*

Pepi II *ruled Egypt for 94 years – the longest reign in history!*

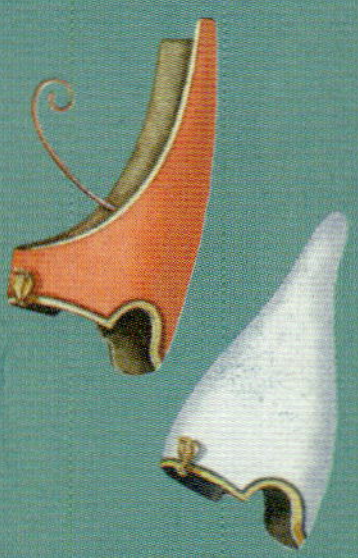

The two royal crowns *were worn together.*

The great pyramids

The three pyramids at Giza are more than 4500 years old. They were built for three kings: Khufu, Khafre and Menkaure. After the kings died, their bodies were preserved as mummies and buried inside the pyramids. Many pyramids still stand today. The biggest one of all, the Great Pyramid, took more than 20 years to build.

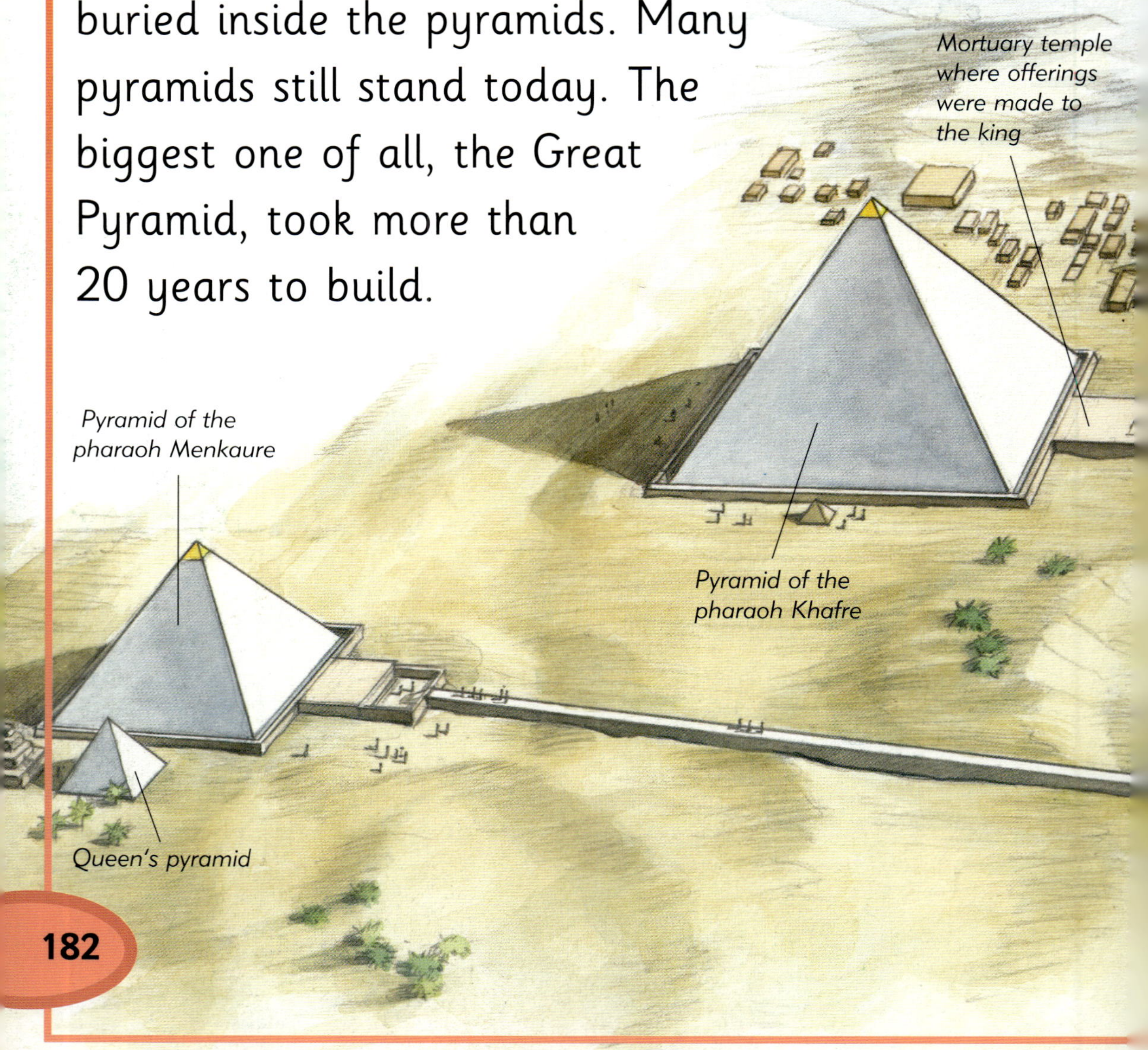

The Step Pyramid *is one of the world's oldest pyramids.*

The Great Sphinx at Giza *is a huge stone statue that is half lion, half human. It guards the way to the Great Pyramid.*

Cleo's fun facts!

A special guide for tomb robbers gave details of fabulous treasures hidden inside the pyramids!

How to make a mummy

Ancient Egyptians were skilled at making mummies. The body's insides were removed, except for the heart. Next, the body was left to dry for 40 days. Then it was washed and filled with linen to keep its shape. Finally, the body was oiled and wrapped in linen bandages.

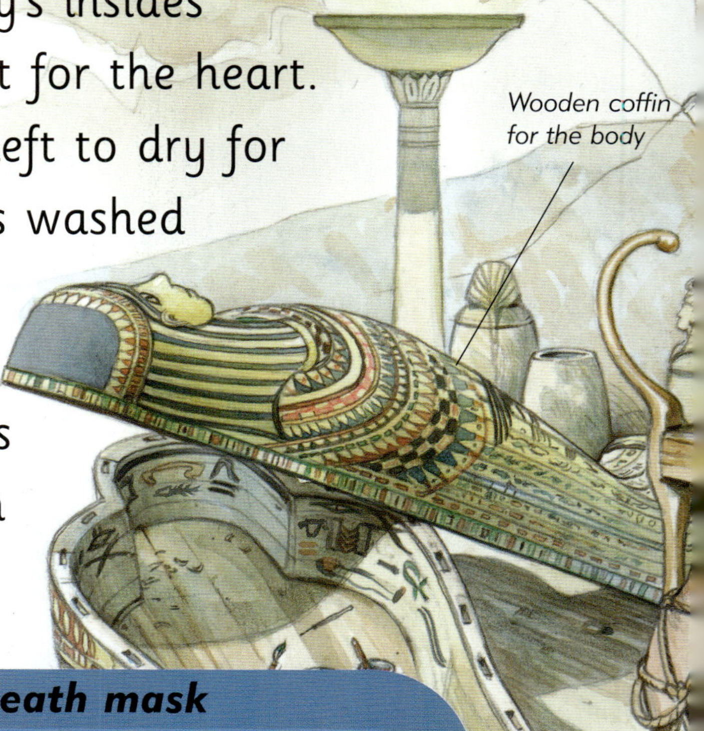

Make a death mask

You will need:

- *play mask (made of plastic or card)*
- *PVA glue*
- *paintbrush*
- *newspaper*
- *poster paints*
- *white paint*

1. *Cover the mask in PVA glue.*
2. *Tear the newspaper into strips. Layer the strips over the mask and leave to dry.*
3. *Cover the mask with white paint. Leave to dry.*
4. *Use the paints to create your own death mask!*

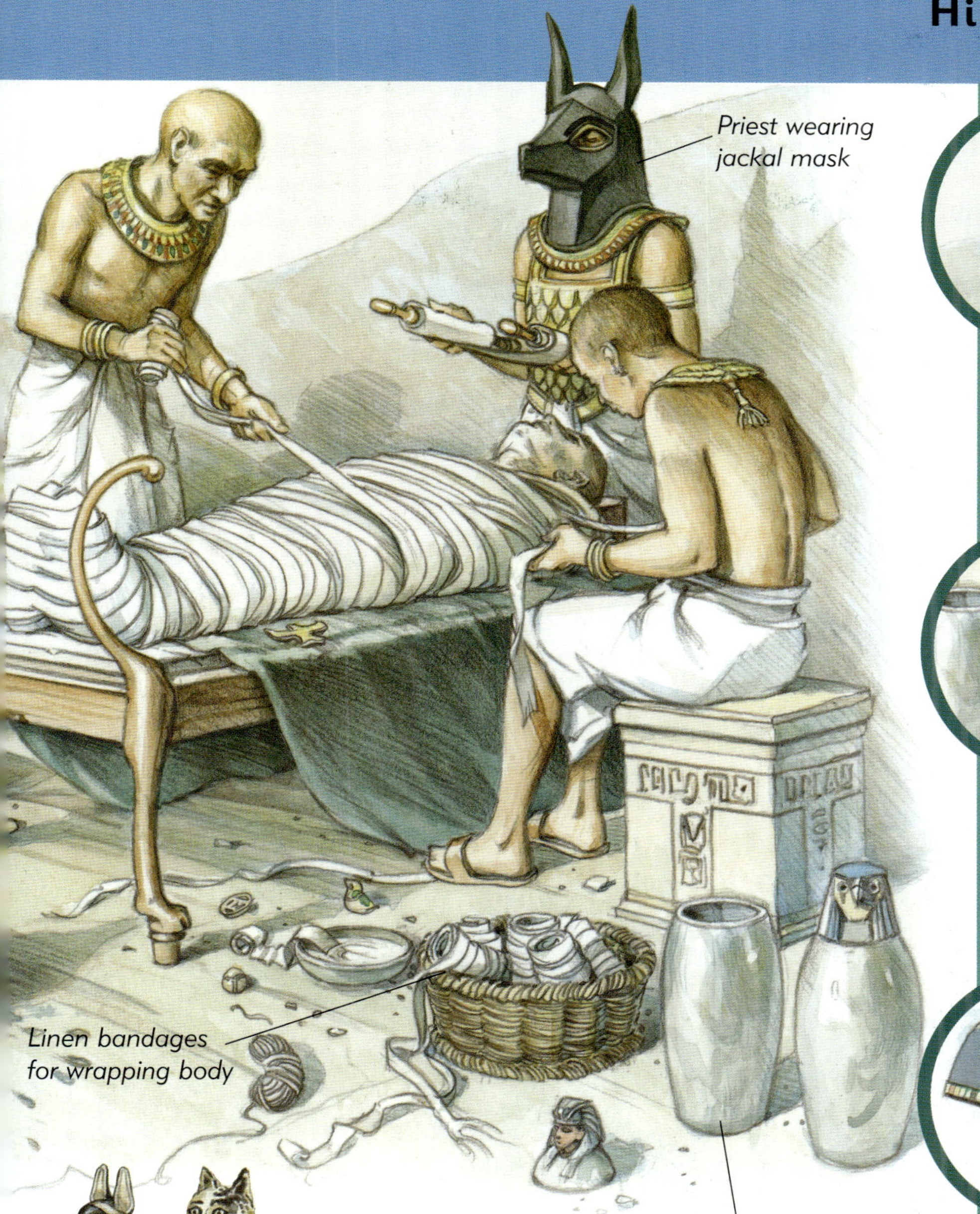

A jackal mask was worn by the priest to look like the god Anubis.

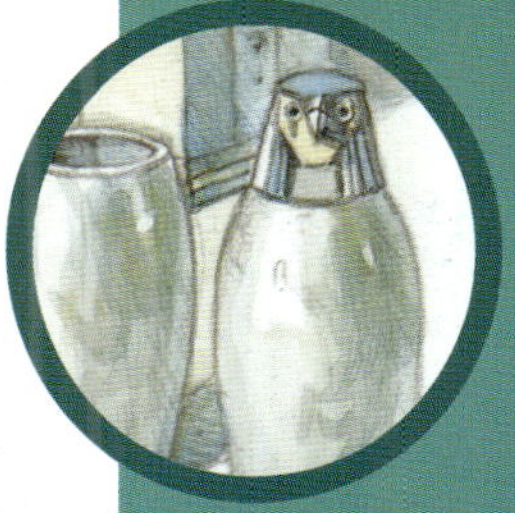

Canopic jars were used to store the dead person's body parts.

Wooden coffins were often shaped like mummies.

◀ *Animals were made into mummies too. A rich man might be buried with a mummy of his pet cat.*

Egyptian know-how

The ancient Egyptians had many skills. They not only invented their own alphabet, but they were the first to write on a kind of paper made from papyrus reeds. The Egyptians also used their knowledge of the stars to help build temples. Egyptian doctors understood the basic workings of the human body.

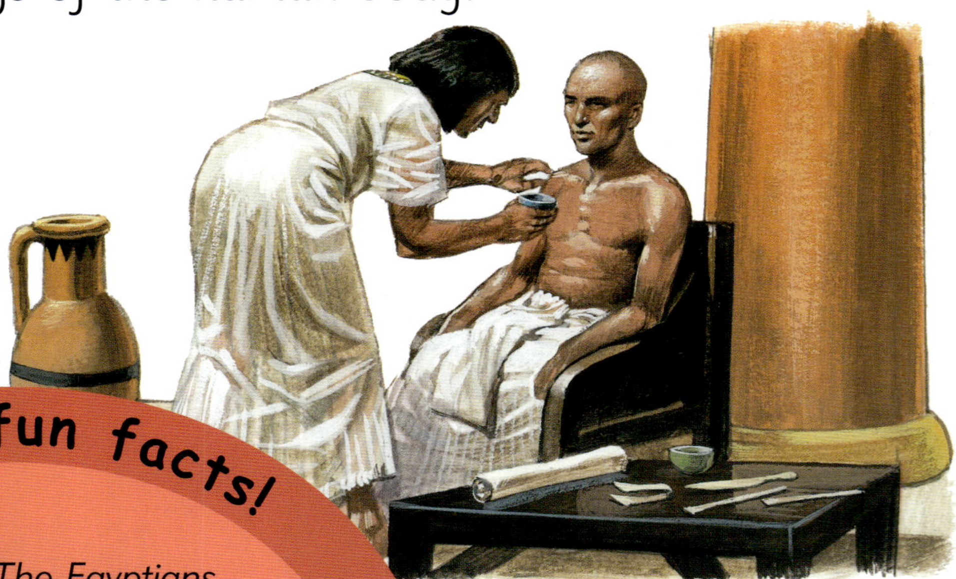

▲ *Egyptian doctors knew how to set broken bones and treat illnesses.*

Cleo's fun facts!

The Egyptians used bulbs of garlic to ward off snakes and to get rid of tapeworms from their bodies!

▼ *Papyrus was expensive because it took such a long time to make.*

1. First people had to cut down the papyrus stems, and cut them into lots of thin strips.

2. Then someone laid these strips in rows on a frame to form layers.

3. The papyrus strips were then pressed under weights. This squeezed out the water and squashed the layers together.

4. Finally, when the papyrus was dry, a man with a stone rubbed the surface smooth for writing.

***Papyrus scrolls** were the first kind of paper ever used.*

***Ink** was made by mixing water with charcoal or coloured minerals.*

***Reed brushes** were used for writing on papyrus.*

Wonder of Greece

The ancient Greeks had many ideas about science, buildings, art, drama, poetry and government. Today, we still feel the influence of these clever people, who lived more than 2000 years ago. The Greeks worshipped gods and goddesses who they believed looked after them in daily life.

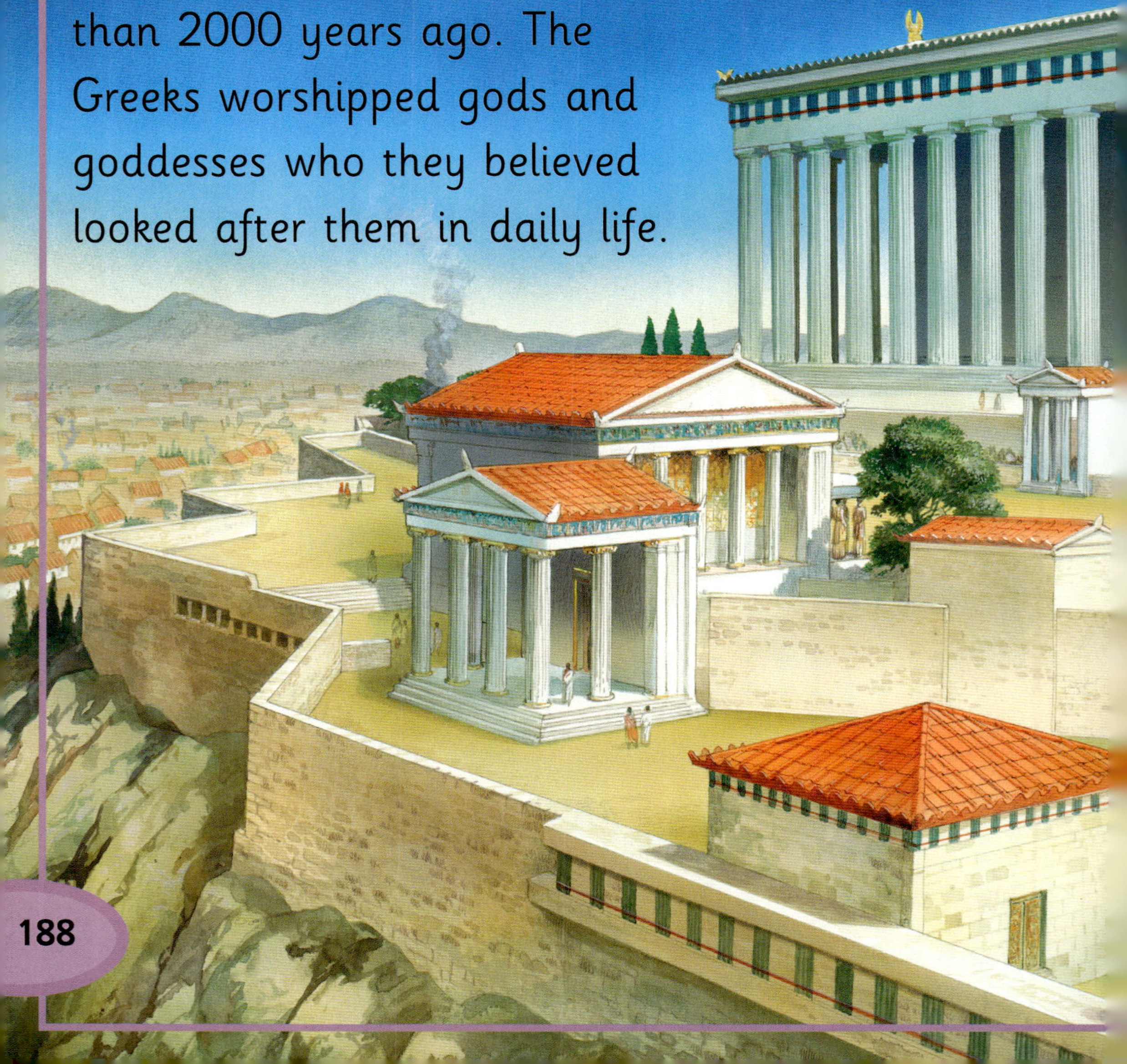

▼ *The Parthenon was a temple built to honour the goddess of wisdom – Athena. Remains of the temple still stand today on the Acropolis, a hill overlooking the city of Athens.*

The minotaur *was a terrible creature from Greek myth. It had the head of a bull and the body of a man.*

Greek soldiers *from Sparta were trained to be very fierce fighters.*

Alexander the Great *was a soldier who once ruled all of Greece.*

People of the East

The ancient Chinese believed that they lived at the centre of the world. They built great cities and canals and learned how to make beautiful silk, paper and pottery. Many of the world's most useful things, such as the compass, were invented long ago in China.

▼ *The first emperor sent hundreds of thousands of workers north to build a great wall to stop fierce tribes from invading China. The Great Wall of China measures over 6000 kilometres in length.*

Make a Chinese fan

You will need:

• A4 paper • colour pens • stapler

1. Take a sheet of A4 paper.
2. Use colour pens to make a Chinese dragon design.
3. Fold the paper into pleats.
4. Staple the bottom end of the fan together.

Fine pottery, such as this horse figurine, was made in ancient China.

Emperors ruled China from 221BC to 1911.

The first compasses were made in China over 2300 years ago.

Rome and its empire

The city of Rome, in Italy, was once the centre of a great empire. An empire is made up of many different countries governed by a single ruler. Rome ruled over 50 million people around the world. The city was busy, noisy and exciting, with many beautiful buildings.

Market stalls were crowded and noisy.

Public fountains provided fresh water from the hills.

Temples were built in honour of the Roman gods.

The people of Rome

By around AD300, Rome was the largest city in the world. Over a million people lived there. The government was run by nobles and knights who were usually very rich. Ordinary citizens, called Plebeians, were quite poor but they could vote and serve in the army. Slaves were not citizens. They could not leave their owners and had no rights.

▼ *The Forum of Rome was the heart of the city. People came here to chat with their friends or have business meetings.*

City guards *protected Rome from outside attackers.*

Senators *were important government leaders.*

Julius's fun facts!

Roman engineers also designed public lavatories. These lavatories were convenient, but not private. Users sat on rows of seats, side by side!

Eating and drinking

Most Romans ate very little during the day. They had bread and water for breakfast and a light snack of bread, cheese or fruit around midday. They ate their main meal at about 4pm. In rich people's homes, a meal would have three separate courses. Poor people ate much simpler foods, such as lentil soup and barley porridge.

Make real Roman food!

PEAR MOUSSE

You will need:

• 1 kg pears, peeled and cored • 6 eggs beaten • 4 tbsp honey • a little bit of oil • $\frac{1}{2}$ tsp cumin • some ground pepper to taste.

1. *Mash the pears together with the pepper, cumin, honey and a bit of oil. Ask an adult to help.*

2. *Add the beaten eggs and put into a casserole.*

3. *Cook for around 30 minutes in a moderate oven.*

4. *Serve with a little bit of pepper sprinkled on top.*

Banquet food *included roast meats, wine and dates.*

Grapes and olives *were popular Roman food.*

A silver jug *like this was used by rich people for serving wine.*

A trip to the baths

Romans baths were more than a place to get clean. They were also places to relax, meet friends and get fit. Visitors could take part in sports, such as wrestling, do exercises, have a massage or a haircut. They could buy scented oils and perfumes, read a book or eat a snack. Or they could admire works of art in the baths' own sculpture gallery!

▶ *There were public baths in most districts of Rome. They were built by Roman emperors or rich families.*

Julius's fun facts!

Although the Romans liked bathing, they only visited the baths once in every nine days!

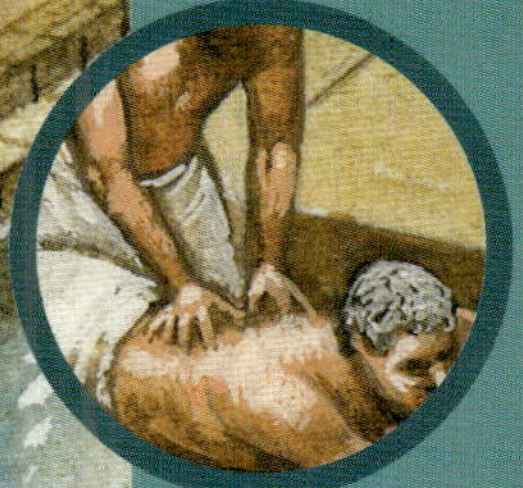

A massage *was the perfect way to relax.*

Men's baths *were separate from the women's.*

Washing *was done without soap. Romans scraped the dirt off instead!*

Having fun

▼ *All the parts in Roman plays were played by men.*

The Romans liked music and dancing. They played instruments such as pipes, cymbals and horns. The Romans also enjoyed going to the theatre to see comedies. They also invented mime, a story told without words through gestures and dance.

Buskers played in the streets or could be hired for parties.

Masks were often worn by actors to help identify the characters.

Julius's fun facts!

Roman actors were so popular that women couldn't sit near the stage, in case they tried to arrange a date with one of the stars!

Gladiator games

Gladiator fights were popular with the Romans. People admired gladiators for their strength, bravery and skill. But gladiators' lives were short and their deaths were horrible. They were sent to the arena to fight until they died. Most did even not choose to fight. They were either criminals or prisoners-of-war.

▶ *The Colosseum was the largest amphitheatre (circular building) in the Roman empire.*

Wild beasts were brought from far away to be killed by gladiators in the arenas.

Chariots were used for racing around race-tracks called 'circuses'.

Julius's fun facts!

Some gladiators became so popular that people wrote graffiti about them on the walls of buildings around Rome!

Roman roads

Rome's first main road was built in 312BC. All roads led to Rome. The city was at the centre of a network of roads that stretched for over 85,000 kilometres. They had been built to link far-away parts of the empire to Rome, so that Roman armies or government leaders could travel more easily. To make travel as quick as possible, roads were built in straight lines, taking the shortest route.

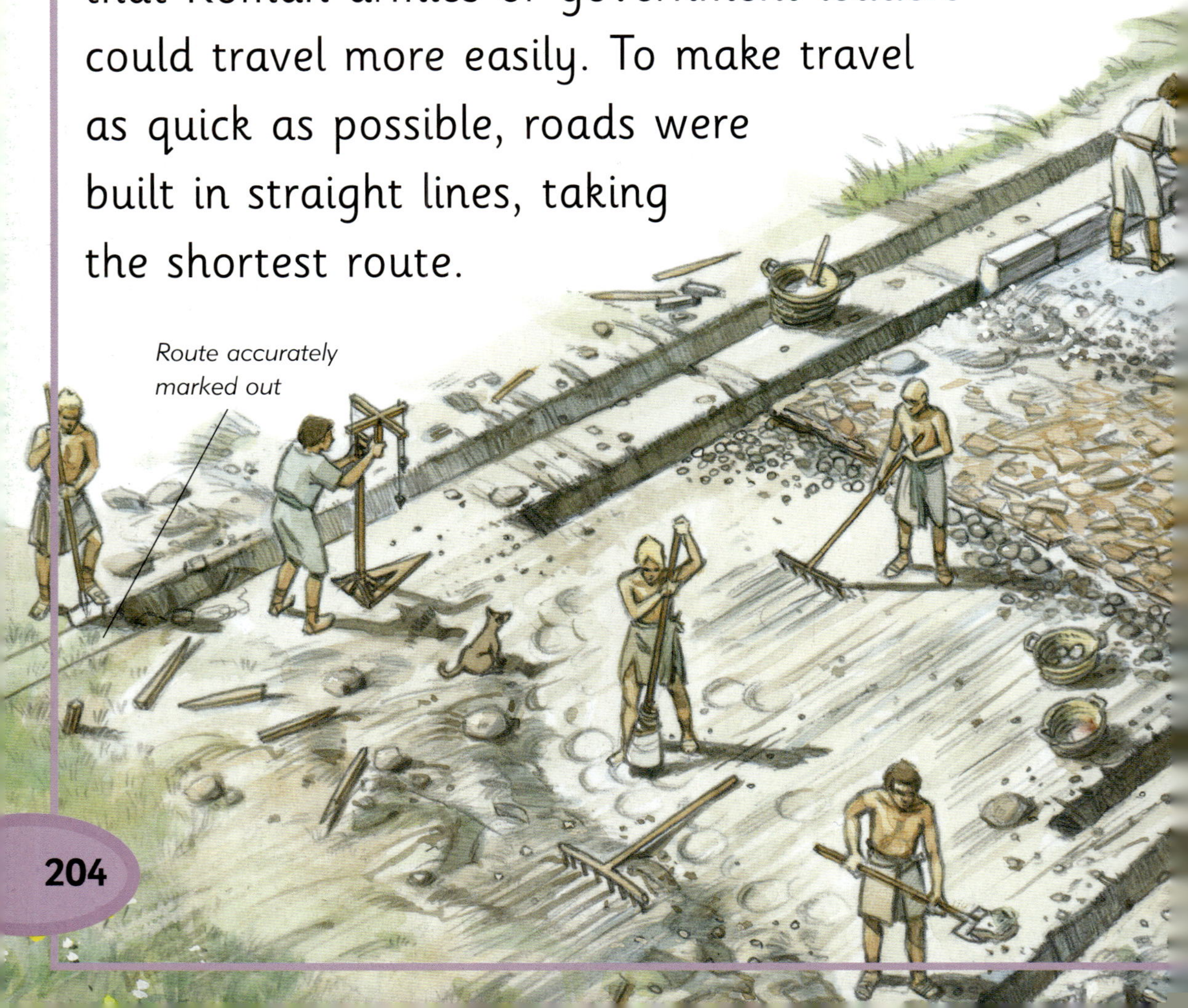

A road engineer *used a 'grome' to measure straight lines.*

Stone slabs *were carefully fitted together for a smooth road surface.*

Julius's fun facts!

The Romans would often consult a fortune-teller or a priest before setting out on a long journey.

Sea raiders

Ancient Greece was home to some of the earliest-known pirates. From around 500BC, there were many cargo ships trading along the Mediterranean coasts, which were often raided by pirates. A few centuries later, the Vikings arrived on the coast of Britain in search of riches and adventure.

▶ *Vikings from the North raided settlements on the British coast. They terrified Britons with their fierce weapons.*

Pirate puzzle

This Greek ship called a trireme was used to fight pirates. It has three banks of rowers on each side. Count them up and see how many were needed to push the trireme along.

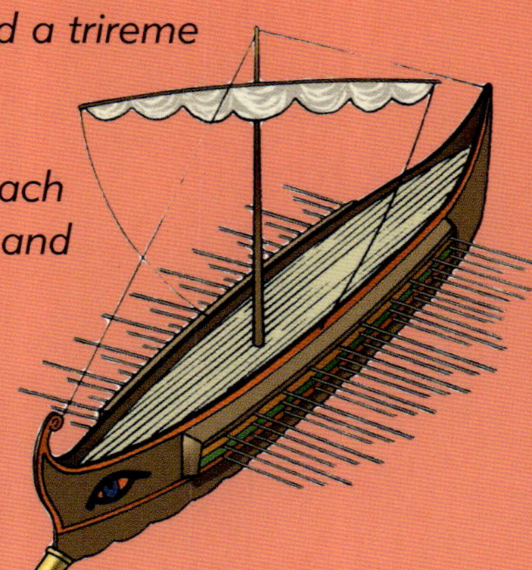

60 rowers powered this ship.

Ancient pirate ships *were small and fast so they could escape easily.*

Roman cargo ships *sailed close to the coast, so it was easier for pirates to attack them.*

Viking longships *were narrow so they could land almost anywhere.*

Amazing Americas

Explorers have discovered ruined cities deep in the rainforests of South America and Mexico. In fact, there had been splendid civilizations in the Andes Mountains and thick forests of Central America for thousands of years. The Incas and Aztecs were two of these ancient peoples. They were great builders, farmers and craftworkers.

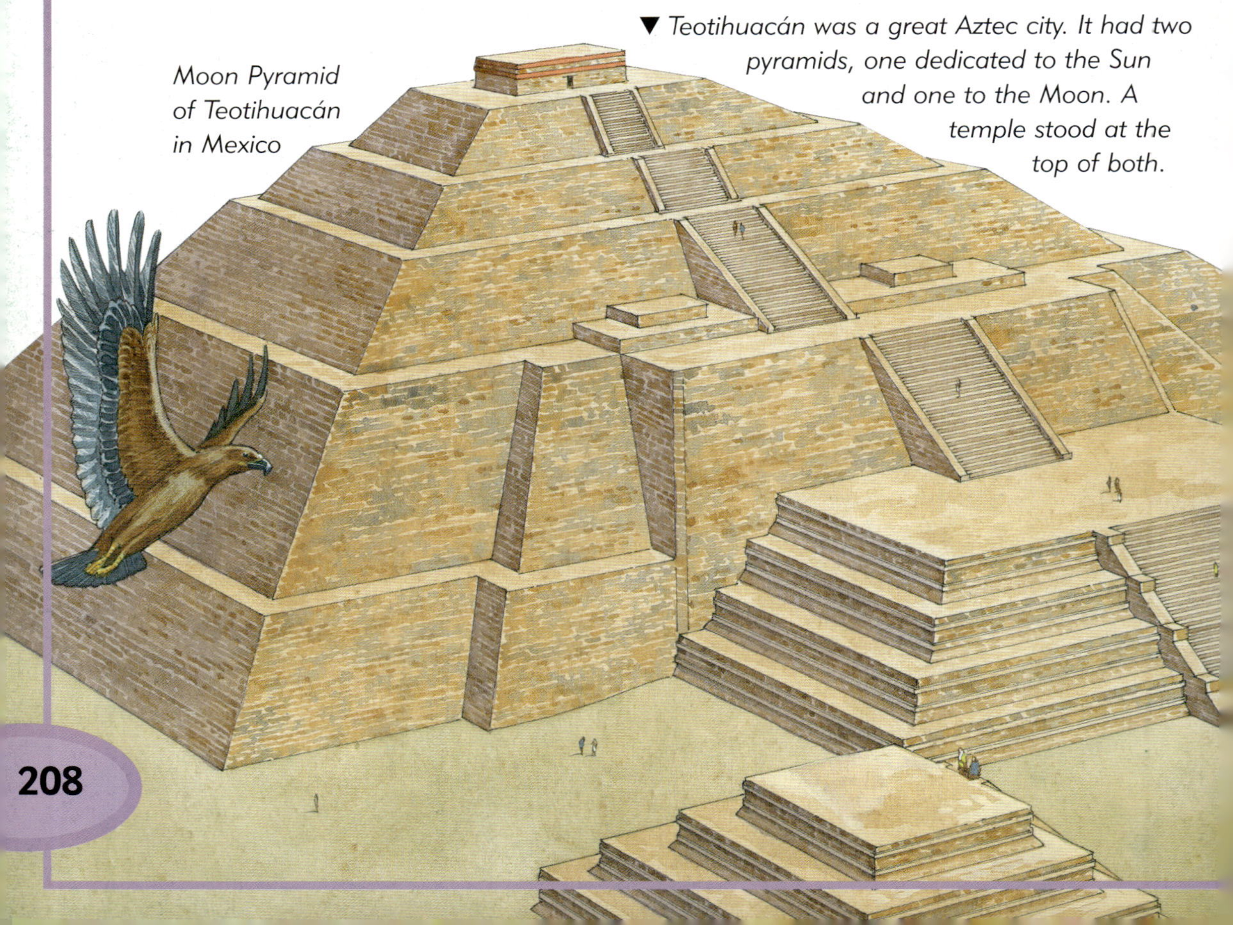

Moon Pyramid of Teotihuacán in Mexico

▼ *Teotihuacán was a great Aztec city. It had two pyramids, one dedicated to the Sun and one to the Moon. A temple stood at the top of both.*

▼ *Machu Picchu was a city on a mountain top in South America, probably built at the end of the 15th century. It had terraced gardens, a temple and a fortress. The abandoned city was rediscovered by an American explorer, Hiram Bingham, in 1911.*

Masks *were often worn for festivals by peoples in the Americas.*

Decorated knives *were used to kill captives as offerings to the gods.*

Central Americans *played a fast, exciting ball game called tlachtli.*

Life in the Middle Ages

In the Middle Ages, between the years 470 and 1450, many castles and forts were built. A castle provided shelter for a king or a lord and his family, and helped him to defend his lands.

Soldiers *practised their fighting skills in the castle grounds.*

Knights *were soldiers who fought on horseback.*

Peasants *farmed the land around the castle.*

The first castles

The first castles were mostly built from wood. But they were not very strong and caught fire easily, so from around 1100 onwards, people began to build castles in stone. A stone castle gave better protection against attack, fire, cold and rainy weather.

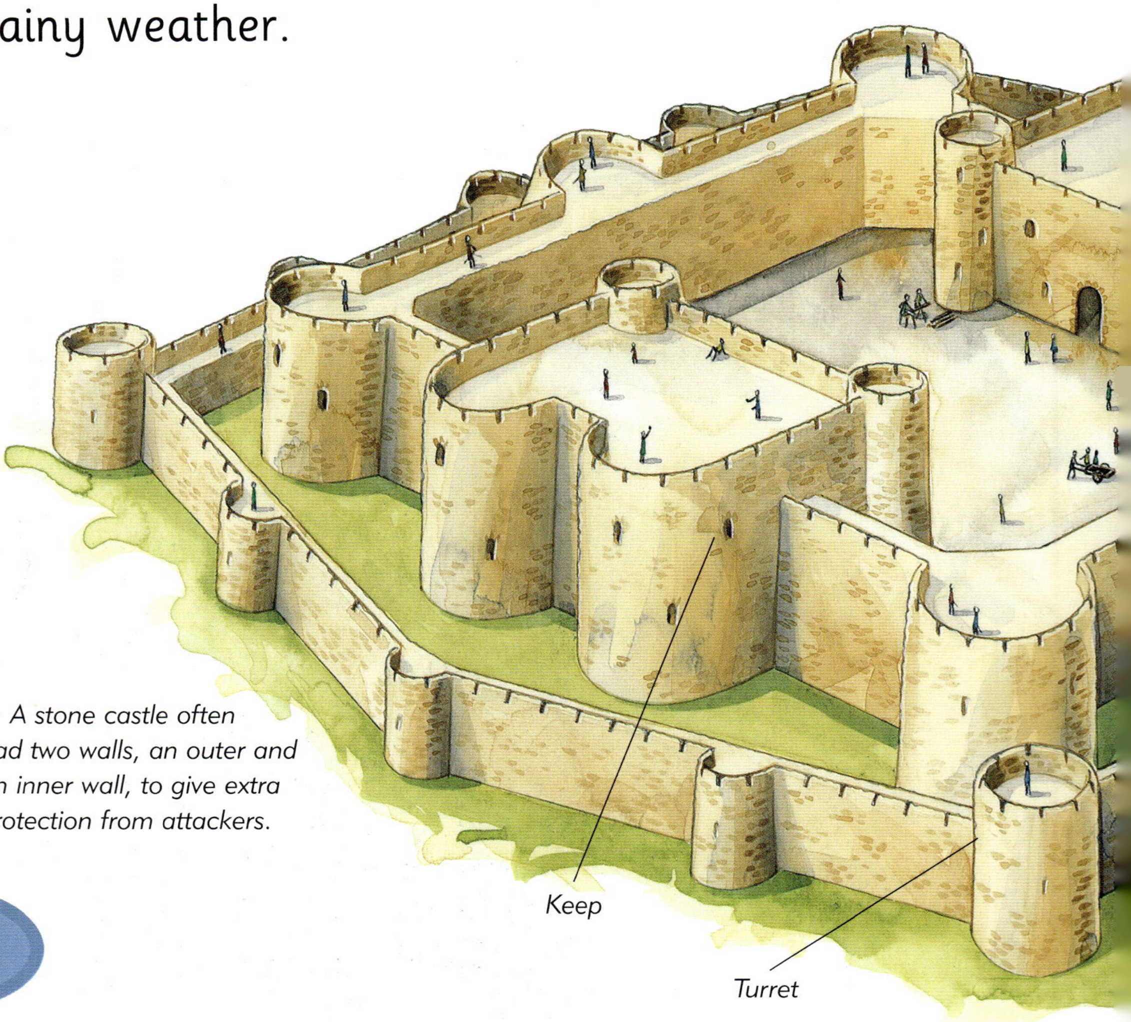

▶ *A stone castle often had two walls, an outer and an inner wall, to give extra protection from attackers.*

▶ *This is a motte and bailey castle. The hill was called a motte, and the courtyard at the bottom was called a bailey.*

▲ *Castle builders dug a deep ditch, called a moat, around the outside of the motte and bailey. This was to stop attackers reaching the castle walls.*

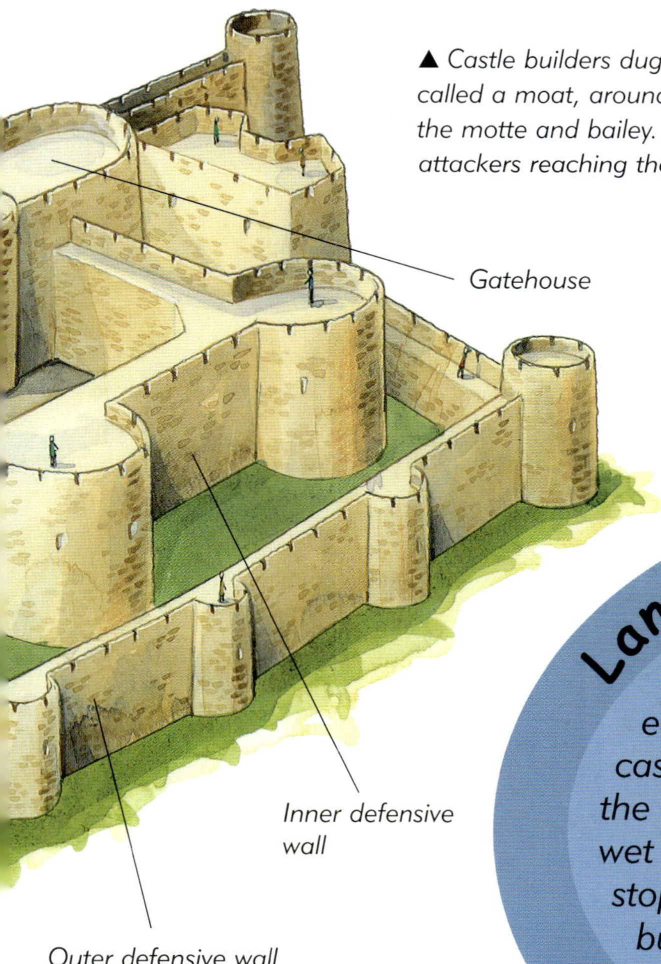

Archers *stood on the castle walls and fired down at enemies.*

Japanese castles *were built with different layers.*

Lancelot's fun facts!

The builders of the early wooden castles covered the walls with wet leather – to stop them from burning down.

People and power

In the Middle Ages, the king or queen was the most important person in the country. The king gave land to his barons and other noblemen. In return, they supplied the king with soldiers and weapons to fight wars. This system of giving away land in return for services was known as feudalism.

Test your memory!

1. *When were the Middle Ages?*
2. *What is the name of the ditch that surrounds a castle?*
3. *What were the first castles made of?*
4. *What was the courtyard at the bottom of a castle called?*

1. between AD470 and 1450 **2.** a moat **3.** wood **4.** the bailey

▲ *In the Middle Ages, the Church and the ruler of the country were both very powerful, so they had to try to work together.*

Barons *were the most powerful of all noblemen.*

Knights *defended the king and lords from their enemies.*

Peasants *were the very poorest people.*

The Crusades

The Crusades were military expeditions from Europe to Palestine, in the Mediterranean. Muslim Turks had seized control of Palestine. European Christians, known as the Crusaders, set out to recapture Palestine from them.

Lancelot's fun facts!

A Crusader knight would share his tent with his beloved horse – it must have been a bit of a squeeze!

◄ The First Crusade set off from Europe in 1096. Between 1096 and 1204 there were four separate Crusades.

Saladin *was a Muslim leader who fought against the Crusaders.*

Richard the Lionheart *was an English king who led the Third Crusade.*

Arab fortresses *like this one at Krak in Syria were taken over and rebuilt by the Crusaders.*

Cruel corsairs

Pirates of the Mediterranean were known as 'corsairs'. The most famous corsairs were Muslims from the Barbary Coast of North Africa. They took great delight in plundering Christian ships. They wanted people, not treasure, so that they could sell them as slaves.

Patch Jack's fun facts!

The famous Barbarossa brothers were so-called because of their red beards – Barba rossa means 'Redbeard' in Latin.

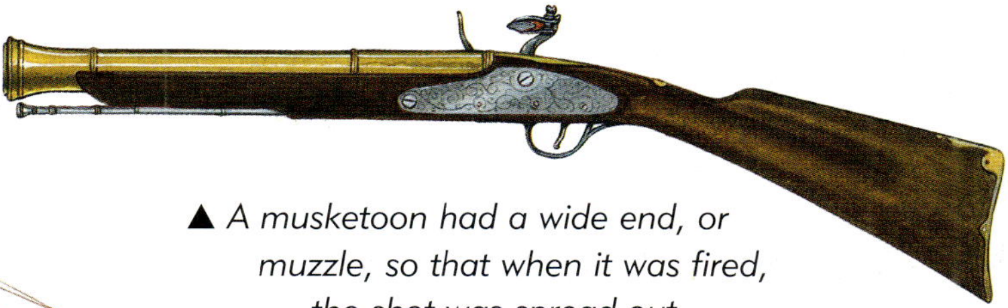

▲ *A musketoon had a wide end, or muzzle, so that when it was fired, the shot was spread out.*

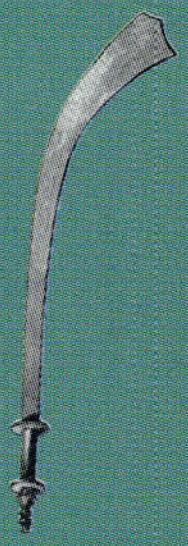

A scimitar *was a curved sword used by the corsairs.*

Grenades *were thrown on to the ship to set it on fire.*

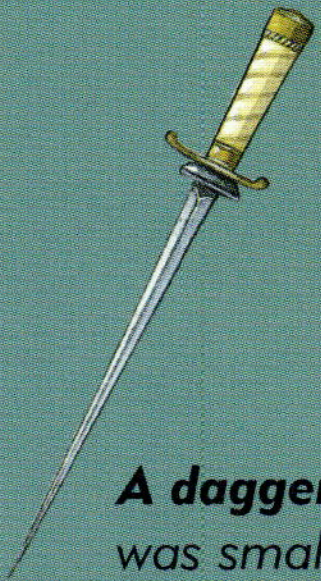

A dagger *was small enough to hide under clothes for a surprise attack!*

Eastern warriors

Warrior knights in Japan during the Middle Ages were known as samurai. The samurai, like European knights, usually fought on horseback but later on they began to fight more on foot. Other Eastern warriors included the fierce Mongols, and the Seljuk Turks who conquered many lands.

▼ *Mongol warriors terrified the enemy in battle. They were skilled horsemen who controlled their horses with their feet while standing up in the stirrups.*

Samurai warriors *wore metal armour fixed to padded silk or leather.*

A curved samurai sword *was a samurai warrior's most important possession.*

Lancelot's fun facts!

The Turks fought with gold pieces in their mouth – to stop the Crusader knights from stealing their gold!

Famous battles

On and off between 1337 and 1453, England and France were at war. This was called the Hundred Years' War. The two countries fought each other to decide who should control France. In the end the French won, and England lost all of her lands in France except for the port of Calais.

▼ *In 1429, a young French girl called Joan of Arc led the French army to victory against the English.*

▲ *The Bayeux Tapestry tells the story of the Norman invasion of England in 1066. William of Normandy, known as William the Conqueror, invaded England and defeated Harold, the English king, at the Battle of Hastings.*

William the Conqueror *claimed that he was promised the throne of England.*

Knights *fought many bloody battles in the Hundred Years War.*

Lancelot's fun facts!

If you captured a knight alive during battle, you could offer him back to his family in return for a generous amount of money!

Dress for battle

Early knights wore a type of armour called chainmail. It was made of thousands of tiny iron rings joined on to each other. Gradually, knights began to wear more and more armour, until by the 1400s, they were wearing full suits of steel armour.

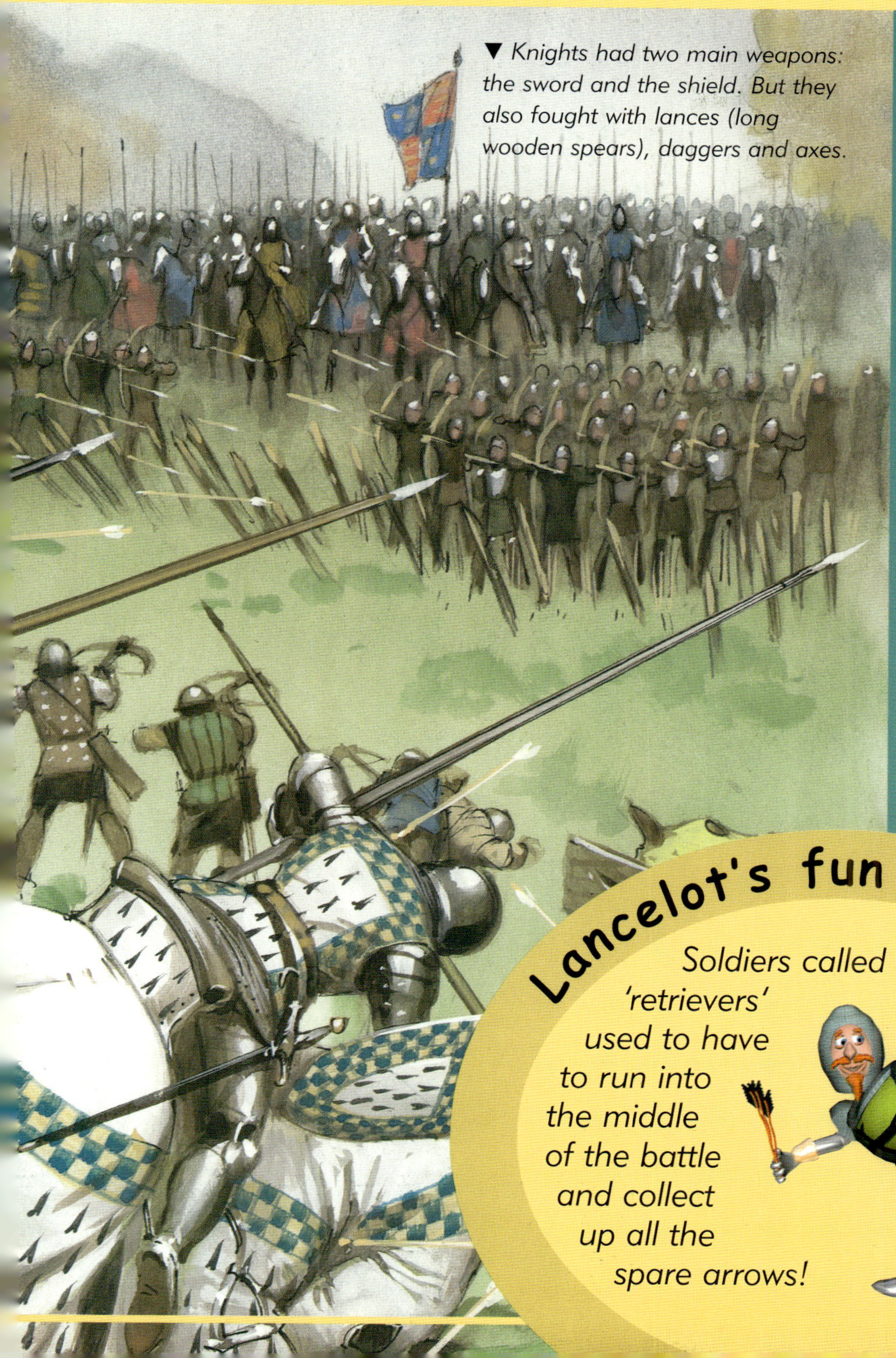

▼ *Knights had two main weapons: the sword and the shield. But they also fought with lances (long wooden spears), daggers and axes.*

A wool tunic *was worn over the top of a knight's armour.*

Chainmail *was a kind of 'knitted' metal armour.*

Lancelot's fun facts!

Soldiers called 'retrievers' used to have to run into the middle of the battle and collect up all the spare arrows!

Spanish invaders

From the early 1500s, Spanish galleons carried vast amounts of treasure across the Atlantic Ocean. Loaded with gold, silver and other riches from Central and South America, these huge ships attracted pirates like bees to a honeypot.

▲ *These soldiers were called* conquistadors. *They were the first Spanish soldiers to invade the 'Spanish Main', or Central and South America.*

Francis le Clerc *was a fierce pirate known as 'Peg Leg' because of his wooden leg.*

Ancient riches *like this gold knife were found in the Americas.*

Patch Jack's fun facts!

When Christopher Columbus, the Italian explorer, first landed in the Americas, he thought he had found Asia!

Ocean of thieves

Pirates sailed the Indian Ocean for many centuries. They were attracted by the exotic treasures of the East, such as silks, spices and jewels. Pirate ships lay in wait along the Indian coast, seizing the cargoes of lone merchant ships as they passed.

Pirate search!

The surnames of five pirates and privateers are hidden in this letter square.

Can you find them all?

B	R	N	A	D	C	X	M
D	R	A	K	E	B	N	O
L	E	C	L	E	R	C	R
K	R	K	S	E	S	W	G
L	O	I	A	A	I	G	A
D	S	D	N	L	S	G	N
C	Y	D	T	E	A	C	H

Drake, Raleigh, Morgan, Le Clerc, Kidd

▼ *The large island of Madagascar was wild and unexplored, so it was easy for pirates to hide there.*

William Kidd *was sent to chase pirates in the Indian Ocean but soon became a pirate himself!*

Precious jewels *such as rubies and emeralds were taken from passing Indian ships.*

Henry Avery, *known as the 'Arch Pirate', captured the Indian Emperor's treasure ship.*

Bold buccaneers

Buccaneers were pig hunters and criminals who had settled on the island of Hispaniola (modern Cuba). The Spanish tried to drive them away, so the buccaneers banded together and started attacking passing Spanish merchant ships.

▼ *The buccaneers invented a special kind of sword – the cutlass. They carried it as their main weapon in battle.*

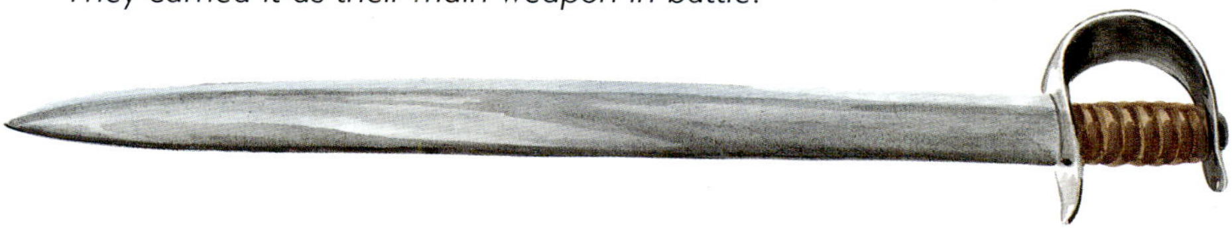

Pirate puzzle

There are six pirate weapons hidden in this picture.

Can you find a scimitar, a dagger, a pistol, a musketoon, a battle axe and a firebomb?

Henry Morgan *started out as a privateer, but soon became a famous buccaneer.*

A battle axe *was used to cut down the sails of the enemy ship.*

A pistol *was light and easy to carry during an attack.*

Attacking the enemy

Some sailors were given permission to attack ships from enemy countries. This could only happen if they carried a special letter from their king or queen. These sailors did not call themselves pirates, but were known as 'privateers'. Privateering mostly took place between the 16th and 18th centuries.

▲ *Francis Drake, a famous privateer, raided Spanish settlements in Panama, Central America. He once attacked a mule train carrying silver.*

▲ *Some privateers captured slaves and sold them in exchange for gold, silver and pearls.*

Walter Raleigh *was beheaded by James I for returning from two voyages empty-handed.*

Francis Drake *was a great privateer, who brought back many riches from all over the world.*

Patch Jack's fun facts!

A ship would raise its country's flag to other passing ships. So privateers often raised a fake flag to an enemy ship to pretend they were friendly!

The high seas

Pirates are sailors who attack and board other ships to steal their cargoes. Their golden age was during the 1600s and 1700s. This was when ships carried treasures, weapons and goods back to Europe from the Americas, Africa and Asia.

▶ *Piracy was a man's world but some women pirates also took to the high seas. Two women, Mary Read and Anne Bonny, were part of a crew that sailed around the Caribbean.*

▶ *The bed of the Caribbean Sea is scattered with the remains of Spanish galleons, many of which still hold treasure.*

Pirate flag!

You will need:

- *paper* • *paints*
- *brushes*

The skull-and-crossbones is the most famous pirate flag, but it was not the only one. Use your paints and brushes to copy one of these designs!

Stolen weapons *were used by pirates on raids.*

Rigging *was often used to climb up and adjust the sails.*

Women pirates *wore men's clothes and used fighting weapons, such as daggers.*

Life in the West

North America is a huge continent. Early settlers and explorers arriving on the east coast moved steadily into the West to fill the huge, empty spaces. They cleared wilderness for farms, dug mines and built towns and railroads. Life was often harsh, with fights over cattle and land – this is why we remember it as the Wild West.

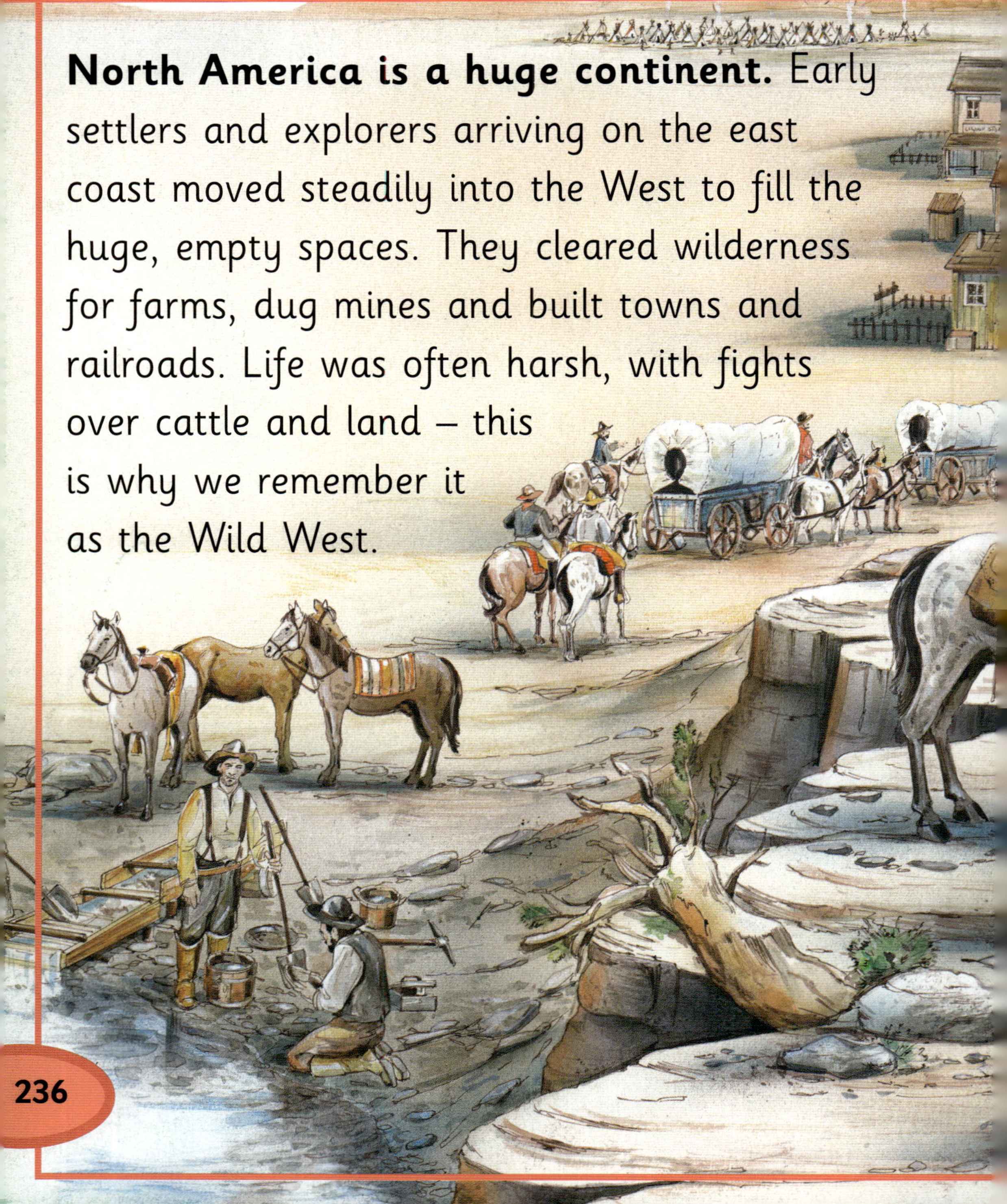

Native Americans *built tepees (tents) out of buffalo skin.*

Wagon trains *were a cheap way of travelling to the West.*

The arrival of horses *from Europe made it easier to catch buffalo.*

New settlers

More and more people came to the Wild West. The government saw that railroads would attract more settlers. A company from the East and one from the West began laying tracks that would join up to form the first railroad across North America. The Homestead Act of 1862 also brought a flood of new settlers to the Plains.

▼ *In 1869, the two railroads that were running across America met in the state of Utah.*

▲ *The Homestead Act of 1862 meant that thousands of people came from the East to set up their own homesteads. Under this law, if you paid ten dollars you could claim 160 acres of land, as long as you stayed for five years.*

Many Chinese workers *helped to build the Central Pacific Railroad.*

Labourers *laid wooden sleepers and metal rails through the wilderness.*

Homesteaders *dug wells, as there was not much water on the Plains.*

The Factory Age

The age of factories and machines began in Europe and North America in the 1700s and 1800s. It is called the Industrial Revolution, a term used to describe the changes brought about when people used steam to make goods. Although factories created many new jobs, pay was low and work was often dangerous.

▶ *In the 1800s, families left the countryside for the city to seek work in new factories. Factory and household smoke made cities dirty places to live.*

Coal became important for fuelling steam engines in factories.

Trains powered by steam were a new way of travelling.

Factories made goods on a large scale.

The world at war

A war fought in many different parts of the world is known as a world war. The first, known as World War One, broke out in 1914 and did not come to an end until 1918. World War Two broke out in 1939 and lasted until 1945. It was the worst war in history, with 55 million soldiers and ordinary people killed around the world.

▶ *British and German fighter planes chased each other during the Battle of Britain in 1940.*

German fighter plane

Word scramble

Unscramble these words to find the different kinds of transport that was used in World War One and Two.

1. ANEPL **2.** KNAT

3. PEJE **4.** RINEMASUB

1. PLANE **2.** TANK

3. JEEP **4.** SUBMARINE

British fighter plane

Big Bertha *was a German cannon that could fire heavy shells more than 15 kilometres.*

Tanks *fought battles in both of the World Wars.*

Foot soldiers, *or infantry, did most of the fighting during World War One.*

Moving on

Without science, we would have to walk everywhere, or ride a horse. Luckily, scientists and engineers have developed many methods of transport, such as the car. Lots of people can travel together in a bus, train, plane or ship.

▲ *Modern airports are enormous. They can stretch for several kilometres, and they have a constant flow of planes taking off and landing.*

▶ *In the airport control tower, air traffic controllers track planes on radar screens. The radar screen shows each aircraft as a blip, with its flight number or identity code.*

Jetways *are walkways that stretch to the plane's doors.*

The passenger terminal *is where people wait for their flight.*

Trains *take passengers to and from the terminal.*

At home in space

A space station is a home in space for astronauts and cosmonauts (Russian astronauts). It has a kitchen for making meals, cabins with sleeping bags, toilets, washbasins and sometimes showers. The space station has places to work and controls where astronauts can check that everything is working properly.

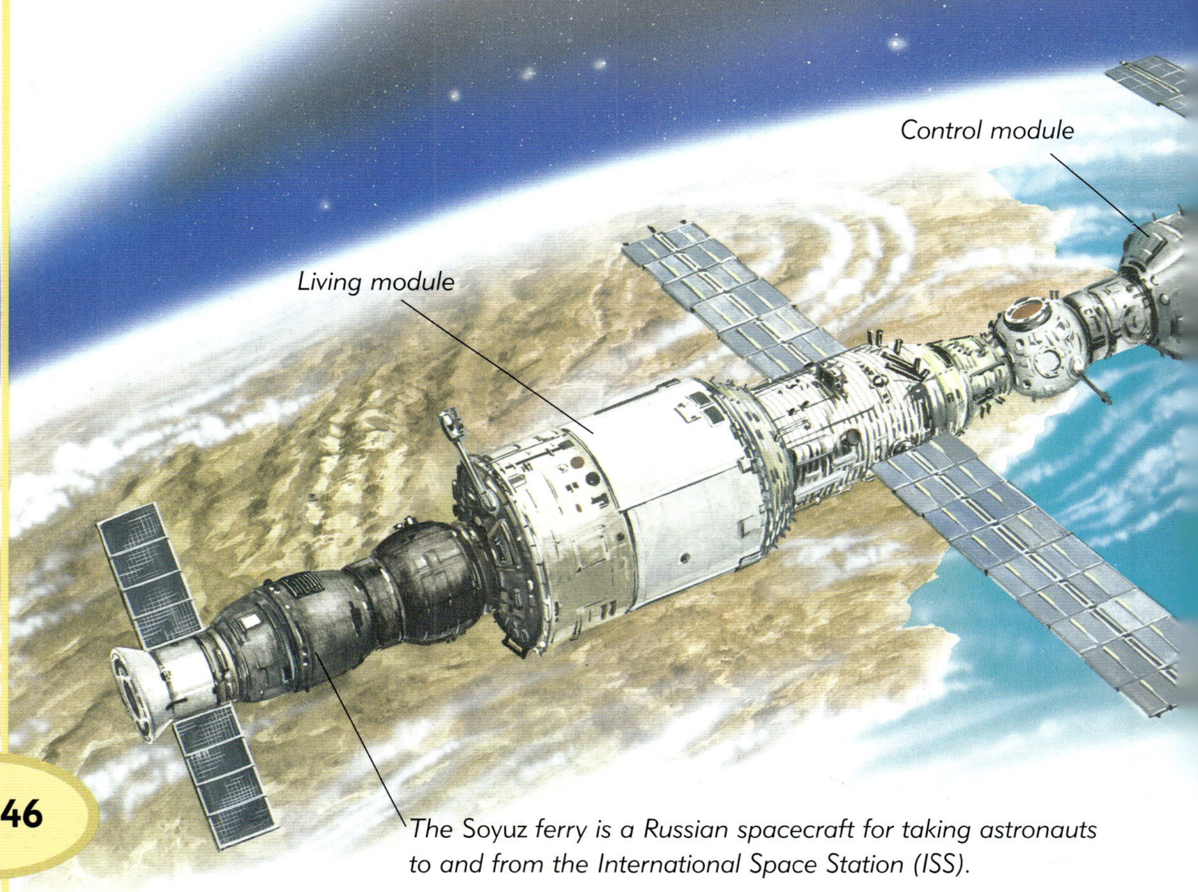

The Soyuz ferry is a Russian spacecraft for taking astronauts to and from the International Space Station (ISS).

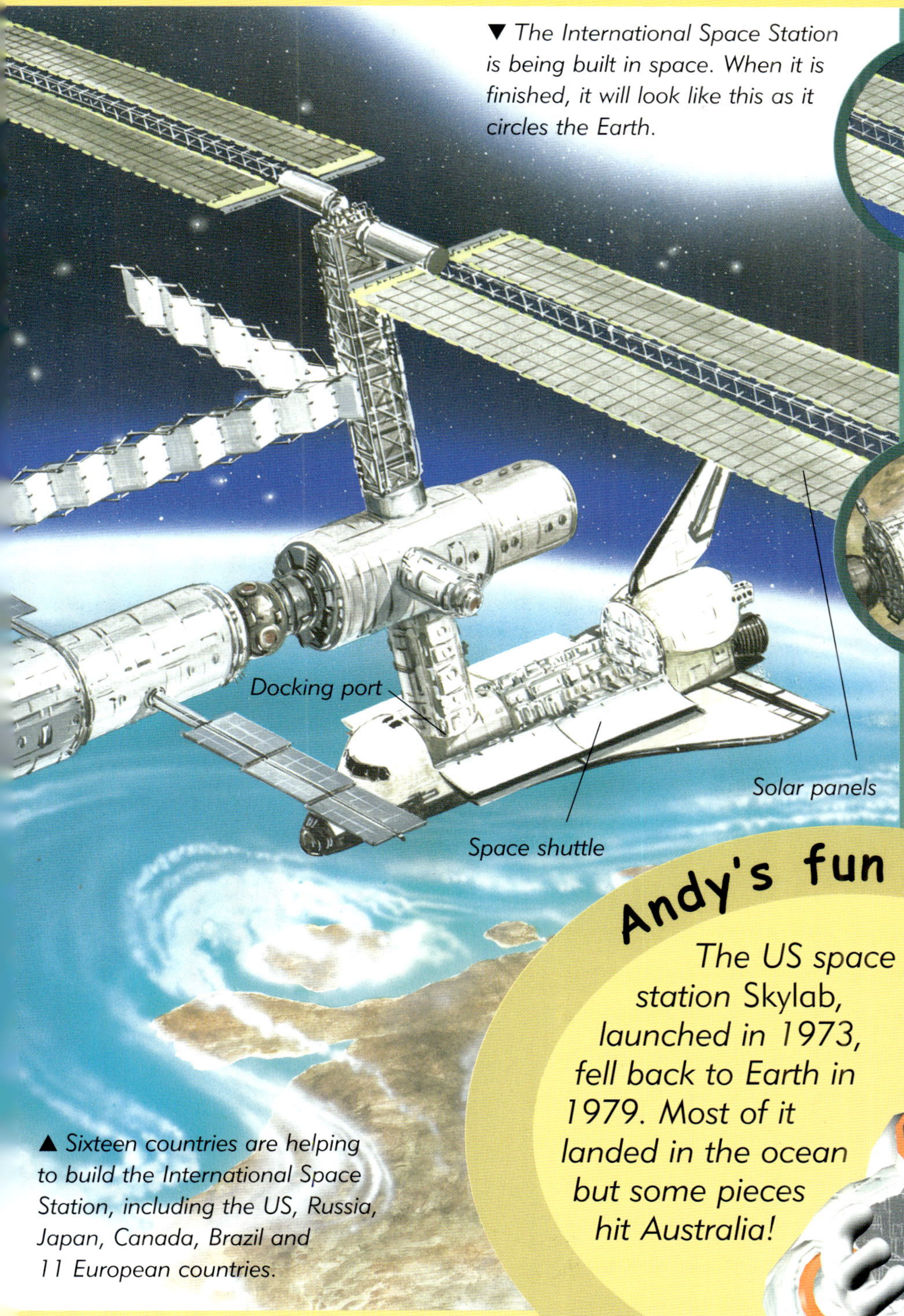

▼ *The International Space Station is being built in space. When it is finished, it will look like this as it circles the Earth.*

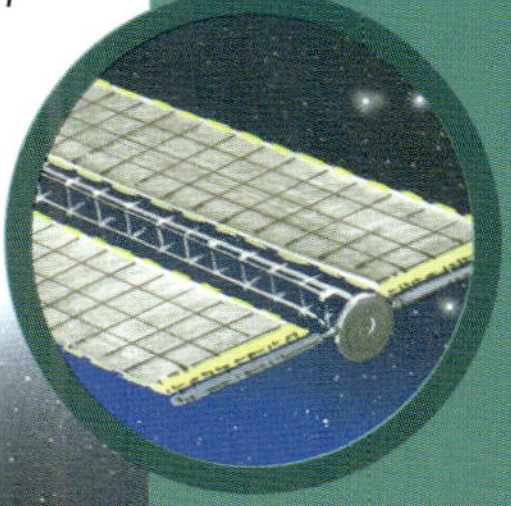

Solar panels *use sunlight to make electricity for the ISS.*

The living module *has room for seven astronauts.*

▲ *Sixteen countries are helping to build the International Space Station, including the US, Russia, Japan, Canada, Brazil and 11 European countries.*

Andy's fun facts!

The US space station Skylab, launched in 1973, fell back to Earth in 1979. Most of it landed in the ocean but some pieces hit Australia!

Index

The numbers in **bold** refer to pictures in your book

Index

Index

Index

ACKNOWLEDGEMENTS

The Publishers would like to thank the following artists
who have contributed to this book:

Susanna Addario (Scientific Illustration), Andy Beckett (Illustration Limited),
Mark Bergin, Richard Berridge (Specs Art), Brett Brecon,
Dave Burroughs (Linda Rogers Associates), Chris Buzer (Studio Galante), Steve Caldwell,
Vanessa Card, Luca di Castro (Studio Galante), Jim Channell/Bernard Thornton Artists,
Kuo Kang Chen, Chris Daunt (Illustration Limited), Peter Dennis (Linda Rogers),
Fiammetta Dogi (Scientific Illustration), Richard Draper, Wayne Ford, Nicholas Forder,
Chris Forsey, Mike Foster (Maltings Partnership), Mark Franklin, Terry Gabbey,
Luigi Galante, Shammi Ghale, Roger Gorringe, Peter Gregory, Brooks Hagan (Studio Galante),
Alan Hancocks, Alan Harris, Sally Holmes, Richard Hook, John James, Julian Baker Illustrations,
Roger Kent, Aziz Khan, Stuart Lafford, Andy Lloyd Jones, Sarah Louise Jones, Angus Mcbridge,
Doreen Mcguiness, Kevin Maddison, Alan Male, Maltings, Janos Marffy, Massimiliano Maugeri
(Studio Galante), Alessandro Menchi (Studio Galante), Colin Newman, Helen Parsley,
Roger Payne, Rachel Phillips, Terry Riley, Steve Roberts, Eric Robson, Eric Rowe,
Martin Sanders, Peter Sarson, Mike Saunders, Rob Sheffield, Francesco Spadoni (Studio Galante),
Nick Spender, Roger Stewart, Graham Sumner (Specs Art), Mike Taylor, Gwen Tourret,
Rudi Vizi, Christian Webb, Steve Weston, Mike White, Tony Wilkins

Computer-generated cartoons by James Evans

www.mileskelly.net
info@mileskelly.net